# TAEKWON-DO

# ACKNOWLEDGEMENTS

I WOULD LIKE TO THANK my instructor, Mr Edmund Chow, for his teaching over the years.

I would also like to thank everyone I have trained with over the years for some great times, memories and bruises(!), especially: Steve Trott, Pete Trott and Sean Hardy, my friends who went with me for that first lesson, after which we all started training, Ian, Paul and Judith Brand, Scott McFarlane, Ho Pang, Laurence Bloom, Dave Francis, Paul Harwood, Alan Clark, Freddie, Ralph, all my students, plus the people I have trained with at Hove and Worthing over the years, and last, but not least, my brother Dan.

Thanks to Ho Pang and Lisa French for taking part in the photography for this book.

Thanks to Nikki for letting me pursue all the avenues that Taekwon-Do has opened up for me.

And, finally, I would like to thank Mick Mitchell, for his advice and encouragement and for getting me started in the martial arts!

PICTURE CREDITS:

The publishers would like to thank the following sources for their kind permission to reproduce the pictures in this book:

Actionplus /Glyn Kirk 15; The Bridgeman Art Library 8; Grand Master Jhoon Rhee 11tr; International Taekwondo Federation 9; Ministry of Culture & tourism of the Republic of Korea/Suh Jae Sik 10tr, 10bl; United Kingdon TaeKwondo Association 11bl

With special thanks to Mr Hyon Tak Hwang at the Embassy of the Republic of Korea, London; Mr Tom Meccallum at the International TaeKwondo Federation, Austria; and Kurn Hong Lee at the World TaeKwondo Federation, Korea, for the time and assistance they have contributed to this project.

Every effort has been made to acknowledge correctly and contact the source and/copyright holder of each picture, and Carlton Books Limited apologises for any unintentional errors or omissions which will be corrected in future editions of this book.

**Project Editor:** Vanessa Daubney
**Project Art Direction:** Mark Lloyd
**Design:** Neil Wallace
**Picture Research:** Debora Fioravanti
**Photographs:** Julian Hawkins
**Production:** Lisa French

Printed in Dubai

In the interests of good health, it is always important to consult your doctor before commencing any exercise programme, especially if you have a medical condition or are pregnant. All guidelines and warnings should be read carefully. The author and publisher disclaim any liability or loss, personal or otherwise, resulting from the procedures and information in this book.

THE FULL COLOUR GUIDE TO THE KOREAN MARTIAL ART

# TAEKWON-DO

FROM WHITE BELT TO YELLOW BELT

JASON CORDER   Black Belt 2nd Dan

CARLTON
BOOKS

# CONTENTS

# INTRODUCTION

I first started my Taekwon-Do training after a brief spell practising Karate. Some friends had told me that they were going to a Taekwon-Do training session in Hove (a town on the south coast of England), not far from where I lived at the time, to see what sort of martial art it was and what a lesson involved. We thought that if we enjoyed it, we would possibly take it up. After meeting the instructor, Edmund Chow, we joined in the lesson and I thoroughly enjoyed it. The power, grace, agility and beauty of this martial art instantly captivated me, and I decided there and then that I wanted to learn more.

Since that first lesson, I have graduated to become a Second Dan black belt, and have competed and been successful in various tournaments and championships. Nowadays, I teach at my own school and I am currently studying for my Third Dan.

This book is aimed at anyone thinking of taking up Taekwon-Do and for those who have just begun lessons. I hope it will help a beginner to understand the techniques involved, as well as some of the theories and the history behind Taekwon-Do.

In here you will find chapters each of which details a different aspect of this explosive martial art, from basic stances, punches, kicks and blocks, to more advanced techniques, sparring and self-defence tactics (one of the main reasons people take up Taekwon-Do). The aim is that anyone starting Taekwon-Do will find a reference to everything they need to know in order to reach the first coloured belt grade which is yellow.

One of the most important things to do, though, is to find a school, and in the initial chapters I explain how to look for a Taekwon-Do instructor and school, how the grading system works and what equipment is necessary.

Respect is an important quality in all martial arts and Taekwon-Do is no exception, so you will also find (in Getting Started) the Taekwon-Do Oath and details of the tenets of Taekwon-Do, which should help you understand the philosophy behind this martial art.

Finally, there is a chapter on relaxing after a training session, a section on how to get further information and a glossary of the Korean words and terms translated into English which are used in this book.

I have found training in Taekwon-Do to be very rewarding and feel that it has made me a better person. It has given me many benefits, including good health, fitness, mental strength, confidence and friends! I cannot imagine my life without Taekwon-Do now and I am sure that if you decide to study Taekwon-Do, then you too will reap its rewards.

JASON CORDER
England, 2001

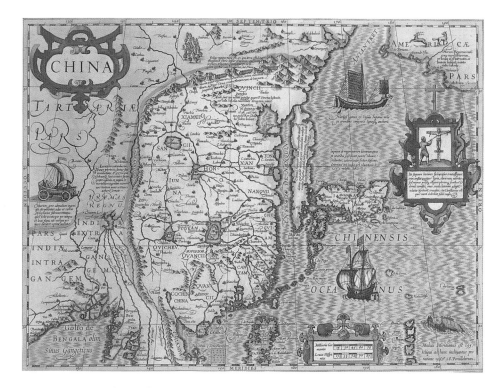

Taekwon-Do is a Korean martial art whose origins can be traced back nearly 2000 years. Translated as 'the way of the foot and the fist', the earliest signs of it in Korean history were found in the Kak-je tomb, where there are drawings depicting two men in a fighting stance, though some people have interpreted it as nothing more than a dance. Whatever the truth may be, what is certain is that there have

# THE HISTORY OF TAEKWON-DO

been numerous martial arts throughout Korea's history, such as *Soo-Bak Do* (or *Soo-Bak Gi* as it is sometimes referred to) and *Tae Kyon*, which were practised in the courts of kings and which formed part of the armies' training. In fact, during the Koguryo dynasty, competitions were held annually, and it was often referred to as foot fighting; while in the sixteenth century, there was a band of warrior youths, which called itself the *Hwa Rang-Do* ('the way of the flowering manhood') and which was similar to the Samurai of Japan, that trained in several arts, including unarmed combat techniques.

These early martial arts were the forerunners of Taekwon-Do and they remained popular throughout the Silla and Koryo dynasties until they started to fade away when the kingdoms went through a period of anti-military rule.

*Grand Master General
Choi Hong Hi*

In 1909, the Japanese invaded Korea and the practice of all martial arts was forbidden. But a general in Korea's army, General Choi Hong Hi, (pronounced 'Chay Hong Hee'), began a personal quest secretly to study and research the old Korean martial arts. In 1938, General Choi went to Japan, where he studied karate, and then after Korea was freed from Japanese occupation in 1945, he started to teach karate to the South Korean Armed Forces. By 1955, General Choi had completed his studies to form a new martial art for Korea, and on 11 April he submitted the name *Taekwon-Do* as the title of the new martial art he had researched. It was accepted, given official recognition, and became part of Korea's culture. The International Taekwon-Do Federation (ITF) was formed in 1966 by the General and this allowed him to set about his personal dream of promoting Taekwon-Do all over the world.

*A nineteenth-century painting depicting a Taekwon-Do contest from the Choson Dynasty*

## What sets Taekwon-Do apart?

In most martial arts, the focus is on the hand, whereas in Taekwon-Do the emphasis is on the leg and kicking techniques, the reason being that the leg is three times stronger than the arm and longer, so providing greater reach. The legs are a human being's most powerful weapons and means of self-defence. Taekwon-Do comprises roughly 70 per cent kicking techniques and 30 per cent hand techniques, all of which are very powerful.

Taekwon-Do is a martial art that is also practised as a sport. Indeed, this aspect of Taekwon-Do has grown significantly over the past 20 years and there are now numerous associations which organize competitions and international and World Championships are held every few years. Those who take part in competitive Taekwon-Do now have to train nearly as often as professional athletes to stay at the top of their chosen discipline.

10

*Most children in Korea take up Taekwon-Do and often give exhibitions like the Green Pine Youth Demonstration Team shown practising here.*

There are three disciplines in the sport:

**Sparring:**   Where two people fight for two-minute rounds on a points-scoring basis. Kicks and punches must be delivered above the waist and to the front of the head and the body.

**Breaking:**   This is a test of strength as well as technique, where a person attempts to break several boards. These boards can be made of hardened plastic which can break and then be put back together, or wood, or sometimes tiles or concrete blocks.

11

**Patterns:**   A pattern is a set series of self-defence moves, which can be offensive or defensive. The idea is to perform the pattern with grace, agility, strength and speed.

Since 1955 the popularity of Taekwon-Do has grown astonishingly. It is now taught all over the world and practised by people of all ages. It is a part of everyday life for Korean people, as natural to them as football is to the British and baseball to the Americans, and it is taught to the Korean army and police force.

Two men have been responsible for the expansion of the art in the west: Master Jhoon Rhee is credited with taking Taekwon-Do to the United States of America. He began teaching the art in America in the 1960s and today he is one of the most respected authorities on Taekwon-Do not only in America, but also throughout the world.

*Grand Master Jhoon Rhee*

Grand Master Rhee Ki Ha brought Taekwon-Do to the United Kingdom. He was the first instructor in England and, along with General Choi, was the instructor who started the first association in England, the United Kingdom Taekwon-Do Association (UKTA).

Even now, General Choi Hong Hi still travels all over the world spreading Taekwon-Do, holding seminars, giving speeches, attending competitions and visiting associations and schools. It is no wonder that Taekwon-Do is now the most popular and practised martial art in the world.

**Finding a School and an Instructor**

Choosing a Taekwon-Do school should be something that you do carefully. The most common places to find a school are leisure centres and sports halls, but you may also find them in church halls, community centres and in schools.

When you visit a Taekwon-Do school for the first time, have a good look round and see what the training environment is like. Is it a friendly atmosphere? Are the students respectful to each other and the instructor? Is the instructor approachable? Does he or she explain techniques to both the higher and lower grades in the class?

# GETTING STARTED

Check to see if the school is part of an association. If it is, then you can usually expect the school to be run efficiently and professionally. There should be regular gradings (see page 15) and competitions to assess improvement, and courses and seminars for you to attend.

Ask the instructor where he or she has trained, and who with, and whether the school focuses on any aspect of Taekwon-Do more than another. For instance, the school could focus on self-defence techniques more than the sporting side or sparring and competing.

You will also need to find out which style of Taekwon-Do is practised at the school. There are two: the ITF style stems from the International Taekwon-Do Federation and therefore directly from General Choi Hong Hi, but there is also the style favoured by the World Taekwon-Do Federation (WTF). ITF Taekwon-Do is more traditional, concentrating as it does on the original theories and ideas of General Choi, and while it does have a big sporting side to it, the WTF emphasises that aspect much more, together with sparring.

If the school has been up and running for a few years, it should have a mixture of grades training there, such as blue belts, red belts and perhaps some black belts, as well as some lower grades with whom you can train. This gives you a sense of how you can improve and something to which you can aspire.

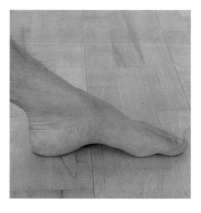

## Equipment and Clothing

To practise Taekwon-Do, you need several pieces of training equipment, but you do not need to buy them all at once. The most important item you need is a training suit, called a *dobok* in Korean, and you should definitely get one in time for your first grading.

There are also several pieces of sparring equipment, which are shown below.

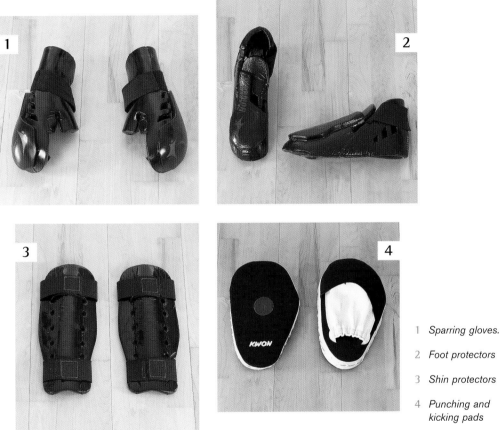

1  *Sparring gloves.*

2  *Foot protectors*

3  *Shin protectors*

4  *Punching and kicking pads*

13

To help students practise techniques and develop more power, they can also use pads, kicking shields and general striking pads. They also help to increase stamina, because while helpful, working with the pads is also quite physical.

Most Taekwon-Do schools should also have a 'breaking horse', which is basically a wooden structure that will hold the boards that are used for performing breaking techniques. The boards are made of hardened plastic and they have a joint down the middle whereby they can slot together and which allows them to be broken, if they are struck with enough speed and force. The idea of board breaking is to develop power and correct technique.

## Belts and the order of rank

The belts in Taekwon-Do each relate to a rank (called *dan gup jedo*) and show the proficiency of each student. To achieve a new belt you must pass a grading (see page 15). There are ten belts from the first, the white, belt, to the ultimate goal of black belt. Each coloured belt level is called a *kup* and each black belt is called a 'degree', or *dan*. The belts are tied round the wearer's waist, since it is believed in the East that the inner power of the human body resides in its centre, which is called the *chi*, therefore if the belt is tied at the waist, then the inner power is kept in. The belts are split with a 'tag' between each one, for example,

*10th kup: White belt*
*9th kup: White belt (yellow tag)*
*8th kup: Yellow belt*

Below is a list of all the belts, in order of rank, and their kup number.

14

*White belt (10th kup)*
*White belt – Yellow tag (9th kup)*
*Yellow belt (8th kup)*
*Yellow belt – Green tag (7th kup)*
*Green belt (6th kup)*
*Green belt – Blue tag (5th kup)*
*Blue belt (4th kup)*
*Blue belt – Red tag (3rd kup)*
*Red belt (2nd kup )*
*Red belt – Black tag (1st kup)*
*Black belt (1st degree / dan)*

## Gradings

These are exams which each student must pass if he or she is to progress to the next belt and level of training. At each grading, there is a set series of moves, techniques and exercises which you must be able to perform correctly, and obviously they get harder the higher up the belts you go. For example, the first grading for the 9th kup white belt – yellow tag comprises a few set exercises, some basic blocks, kicks and punches, and both the four-directional punch (*Saju jurugi*) and the four-directional block (*Saju makgi*). Plus you may also be asked some basic questions about Taekwon-Do and what you have learnt so far.

In comparison, the exam for the 1st kup red belt – black tag entails performing a great deal more, including each pattern (*tul*) that you know, various breaking techniques, and all the kicks, punches, and blocks, kick combinations and self-defence moves that you have learnt. You may have to spar with another student, or possibly do some 2 *versus* 1 sparring, where you must spar against two other students at the same time. And you must know the Korean term for each pattern, kick, punch, and part of the body etc.

A set period of time must expire before you can take your next grading. Possibly, your instructor may feel that you are not quite ready to take the next grading, even though you are eligible and think that you can do it. But the instructor has to be confident that you would do well.

All gradings are performed in front of a panel, which will consist of anything between two and six black belts. They will give their opinions and remarks on your performance to the chief examiner, who will hold the highest dan at the grading. He or she may be your instructor, or perhaps the instructor of your instructor.

Although each association marks students slightly differently, there are usually three levels of passing at a grading: 'A', 'O' and 'L', and there is also a fail mark.

15

### The Taekwon-Do Oath and Etiquette

Etiquette should be observed at all times in the Taekwon-Do *do-jang* (training hall). The instructor should be addressed as Sir, or Miss, or Mr/Mrs… and their surname. On entering and leaving the *do-jang*, you should bow, as a mark of respect. Students must also bow to one another when they are paired up to begin training. The idea is that this mark of respect encourages a good training environment.

General Choi Hong Hi created the Tenets of Taekwon-Do, five principles by which a student should try and live his or her life. The General believes that by following them a student can help to promote Taekwon-Do throughout the world and become a better human being.

16

The tenets are as follows (Korean translations in brackets)*:*

> **Courtesy** (Ye Ui)
>
> **Integrity** (Yom Chi)
>
> **Perseverance** (In Nae)
>
> **Self-control** (Guk Gi)
>
> **Indomitable Spirit** (Baekjul Boolgool)

The other thing that a student should learn is the Taekwon-Do oath. It is usually spoken at the beginning of a class, along with the tenets, by a black belt or a high-ranking student. The student will say a tenet, which the rest of the class then repeats, followed by each sentence of the oath which is shown below.

*The Taekwon-Do Oath*

> I shall observe the tenets of Taekwon-Do
>
> I shall respect my instructors and my seniors
>
> I shall never misuse Taekwon-Do
>
> I shall be a champion of freedom and justice
>
> I shall build a more peaceful world

## The Taekwon-Do Evergreen Tree

The Taekwon-Do evergreen tree is a way of thought for students and instructors. It is a representation of you on the journey of training and learning Taekwon-Do. Throughout your training you grow in strength, ability and knowledge, just as a plant grows into a towering tree, and the colour of each belt represents the Taekwon-Do evergreen tree:

**White** (Huin-Saek) *signifies Innocence – the innocence of the beginner who has no previous knowledge of Taekwon-Do.*

**Yellow** (No-Rang) *signifies Earth – the earth from which a plant sprouts and takes root as the foundations of Taekwon-Do are laid.*

**Green** (Nok-Saek) *signifies Growth – the growth of the plant as your Taekwon-Do skills begin to develop.*

**Blue** (Ch'ong-Saek) *signifies Heaven – the heaven towards which a plant grows into a towering tree as Taekwon-Do skills and training progress.*

**Red** (Pal-Gang) *signifies Danger – the danger that cautions the student to exercise control and warns the opponent to stay away.*

17

**Black** (Kom-Jong) *signifies Maturity – the plant which has now grown into a towering tree and, as the opposite of white, it indicates maturity and proficiency in Taekwon-Do. It also indicates the wearer's imperviousness to fear and darkness.*

The tree is also known as an evergreen tree because it can be interpreted as being 'forever young', a philosophy to which a Taekwon-Do student can easily relate since, in a sense, martial arts training is for ever, because it is something that takes a lifetime to master.

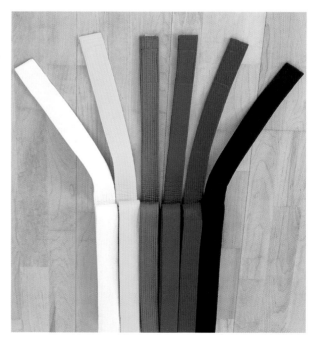

## Warming up

It is very important to warm up your muscles, joints and limbs so that you are able to work to your maximum potential. Every Taekwon-Do lesson should begin with a warm up of some kind. It will usually consist of a wide range of aerobic-type exercises, stamina and balancing exercises, some body conditioning and light stretching. These exercises can be done in sustained periods, or in more explosive repetitions, for example, you might do 30 seconds of push-ups while your partner spots you and then swap round.

18

The warm-up should also be enjoyable, though, and get the class in the mood for a training session. The idea is to get your blood pumping and flowing through your veins ready to train. Once the warm-up has been completed, a class usually moves onto some stretching techniques. Everyone needs to work on stretching, because only a few people are naturally supple, and it is probably more important in Taekwon-Do than in any other martial art, since there are so many kicks which require a high degree of flexibility.

Good warm-up exercises for stamina training include push-ups (good for the upper body, arms and stomach), sit-ups (good for the lower stomach), tuck jumps, that is, standing on the spot and jumping up in the air while pulling your knees up at the same time (good for strengthening the leg muscles), leg raises – lying on your back and raising your legs up straight, and then back down again (good for your stomach), shadow boxing and shadow kicking – throwing punches and kicks as you fight against an imaginary opponent (also good for developing stamina).

Some warm-ups use pads. A more explosive type of warm-up, the aim is to punch, strike and kick the pad for a short burst of time, maybe 30 seconds to a minute. If, however, you are concentrating on building in some stamina exercises into your warm-up, then the pad work will probably last for one to two minutes at a time, which is about the same length as a sparring bout in a competition.

## Terminology

As Taekwon-Do is a Korean martial art, each move and technique has a Korean name and to progress you will need to learn and remember them and other terminology in Korean. Each technique shown in this book gives the Korean term for it, but there is a glossary on page 126 which lists them and below is a list of numbers which may also come in useful.

*Numbers:*

| 1 – **Hana** | 6 – **Yosot** |
|---|---|
| 2 – **Dool** | 7 – **Ilgop** |
| 3 – **Set** | 8 – **Yodol** |
| 4 – **Net** | 9 – **Ahop** |
| 5 – **Tasut** | 10 – **Yol** |

19

# BASIC STANCES

The stance is one of the most important aspects of Taekwon–Do. Your balance, reactions, and body movement are all affected if you do not make sure that your stance is correct.

In the majority of stances that you will learn, it is important to try to keep your back straight. Your shoulders should be relaxed, but your stomach muscles and chest should be tensed. If your stances are correct, then it will be easy for you to move swiftly into attacking and defending positions.

1 *Your feet should be roughly one-and-a-half shoulder widths' apart.*

2 *Keep your back straight while leaning into this stance.*

21

### Walking Stance – Gunnun Sogi

Probably the first stance you will be taught when you take up Taekwon-Do, the walking stance is one of the strongest. It is a good attacking and defensive stance to adopt.

The weight is distributed evenly on both legs, with the front leg bent so that the kneecap forms a vertical line with the heel, while the rear leg is locked out straight. The front foot faces forwards, with the rear foot angled out to about 25 degrees.

( TIP ) *Try to remember not to lean too far forward in this stance, which might cause you to overbalance.*

1 *Sink down into the stance, bending your knees so that your kneecaps come over the front of your feet.*

### Sitting Stance – Annun Sogi

Another strong stance, sometimes known as mountain stance or horse stance, where the weight distribution is spread evenly on each leg and from which it is easy to change quickly into walking stance.

22

Your feet should be one-and-a-half shoulder widths' apart, facing forwards and parallel. The inner thighs are tensed inwards for strength in the stance, and the soles of the feet should grip the floor. Bend your knees forwards until your kneecaps are in a line over the balls of your feet.

( TIP ) *Try not to sit too deeply in this stance, as it can affect your ability to move quickly.*

2 *Make sure your feet remain parallel to each other and that your weight is evenly distributed.*

*Keep your body taut and upright.*

### Attention Stance – Charyot Sogi

Used at the beginning and end of a class, when the class lines up for the beginning of a session or at the end when the students bow, the attention stance is formed by standing with your heels together and both feet facing outwards at an angle of 45 degrees. Your arms should be held slightly in front of you with your fists lightly clenched and your eyes facing front. When you bow, you should bend the body forwards 15 degrees, while you keep your eyes on your opponent as you are bowing.

1 *Make sure that your back is straight and that your legs are locked out.*

## Parallel Ready Stance –
Narani Junbi Sogi

This stance is used when you are waiting to perform an action, or waiting to go into another stance, such as attention stance.

Both feet face forwards in a straight line and one shoulder width apart. Hold your arms in front of your abdomen and chest in a loose circle shape, with your fists slightly clenched, and keep your back straight and your head up.

24

( TIP ) *Do not bend your knees; keep them locked out straight.*

2 *There should be one shoulder's width distance between your feet.*

1   *Keep your front leg ready to defend swiftly.*

### 'L' Stance – Niunja Sogi

The 'L' stance is used very widely in Taekwon-Do, mainly in a defensive manner, as the front foot is readily available for kicking.

Your front leg should carry approximately 30 per cent of your body weight, while your back leg carries the rest. Your legs need to be one-and-a-half shoulder widths' apart, from the footsword (the side of the foot) of the rear foot to the toes of the front foot. The toes of both your feet should be pointing 15 degrees inwards.

25

( TIP ) *Take care not to make this stance too narrow. It's easy to do, and means you will have no balance or stability.*

2   *Lean the majority of your weight back into the stance while keeping your body upright.*

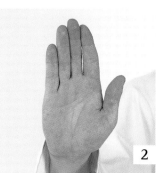

1 Forefist.
2 Palm.
3 Backfist.
4 Inner knifehand.
5 Outer knifehand.
6 Hammer fist.

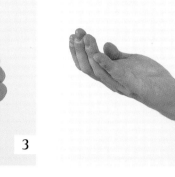

# BASIC PUNCHES

Punches are used in Taekwon-Do, but not to the same extent as kicks. This chapter contains the punches which are most commonly used, showing the correct hand formation and striking part of the fist. Often, you use the first two knuckles of your hand to strike with because they are the most powerful. Obviously it is difficult to kick when standing close to an attacker, which is when punches and hand strikes should be used.

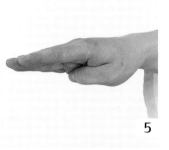

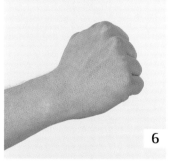

When punching, there are a few things to remember:

1 *Your feet should be planted firmly on the floor at the point of impact, to achieve maximum power through the technique.*

2 *You should twist your hips through the technique in order to generate power, so that you use the strength of your body and not just the strength of your arm.*

3 *You should relax your arm and fist until the moment of impact, at which time you should then tense your body, arm and fist accordingly.*

4 *Use the arm that you are not punching with to guard your head and body.*

*1 This punch is usually performed in walking stance and aimed at your opponent's middle section.*

## Reverse Punch – Bandae Jurugi

The reverse punch is one of the most commonly used punches in Taekwon-Do sparring and self-defence techniques. It generates a lot of power and is usually thrown from the hip, but can be thrown from a higher position, that is, from a high guard, though it is slightly less powerful from that position.

If the punch is thrown with the right hand, your left leg should be forward, and vice versa. This is why it is called the reverse punch. The walking stance is most commonly adopted when a reverse punch is delivered. If the reverse punch is coming from hip height, then the hand that is being used should be in a properly formed fist, with the knuckles facing downwards. As the punch comes up in a straight line from the hip, your fist twists over as it travels and the punch is delivered with the first two knuckles of the fist, which are facing upwards.

Another point to remember is that you should twist your hips into the technique as you step forward and deliver the punch.

( TIP ) *Remember to turn your shoulders and upper body with this punch as you turn your hips.*

*2 Make sure that your punching arm is straight and is aimed at the centre of your target.*

1 *Take care not to overextend yourself with this punch. If you do, you will lose balance.*

## Obverse Punch – Baro Jurugi

Likened to a jab that a boxer uses, the obverse punch is another much used technique in sparring and self-defence. In sparring, it is often used to 'measure' the distance between the Taekwon-Do student and his or her opponent. If the obverse punch can reach, or nearly reach the opponent, then a reverse punch or another technique can be thrown with you knowing that 95 per cent of the time it will make a hit.

When you throw an obverse punch you should have the same leg forward as the hand you use, that is, if you punch with your right hand, your right leg should be forward and vice versa. Again, you should relax until the final moment of impact, when you should tense your body to achieve maximum power on impact.

You strike your opponent with the first two knuckles of the hand, as with the reverse punch, the knuckles should be facing upwards.

( TIP ) *This is a good punch to use when sparring, as it is very quick, and it is hard for your opponent to get round it, particularly if you use it repeatedly.*

2 *If you are punching with your left arm, make sure that you have your left leg forward and vice versa.*

*1 Remember to strike with the first two knuckles of your hand when delivering a hook punch.*

1

## Hook Punch – Dollyo Jurugi

Best used at a slightly closer distance than that of the reverse or obverse punch, the hand position for the hook punch can vary, with some people turning their fist so that the knuckle side faces away from your body as the first two knuckles impact on the target. The other way to throw this punch is with your knuckles facing upwards, with your hand travelling in a horizontal position to the target as the knuckles strike. You arm should come round in an arc as you perform the punch.

29

( TIP ) *This punch can be very powerful when delivered. Remember to turn your hips, upper body and shoulders into it to develop good power.*

2

*2 Bring your punch onto and then through your target. Remember to keep your other arm in a guarding position.*

30

## Side Punch – Yop Jurugi

More a technique for self-defence than a technique for sparring, the side punch is best thrown when you are very close to your opponent or attacker.

The punch can come from the hip or, if you hold your hands a little bit higher than usual, it can come from the centre of your body. The fist is shaped in a horizontal manner, and the first two knuckles are primarily used to make contact with the target.

The side punch should be used when you are standing sideways on to your opponent.

1 *Keep your arm straight and locked out while maintaining a correct fist formation.*

1 *The upset punch is delivered in a slightly upwards circular motion to the lower stomach or groin.*

## Upset Punch
### – Dwijibo Jurugi

This is another punch that is used both for self-defence and sparring.

With the upset punch, the fist remains in its starting shape from the beginning of the move to when it strikes the target, rather than being rotated in the opposite direction, as it is with some punches. Your fist should be horizontal, with the knuckles facing downwards.

Usually aimed at an opponent's stomach (though it can also be aimed at the jaw), the upset punch is best delivered at close or medium range, and it can also be performed as a double punch, especially in a self-defence situation.

31

2 *Keep you other hand in a guarding position as you punch.*

# BASIC
# KICKS

Taekwon-Do focuses on kicking more than any other aspect of the art. Through correct technique, you can generate an incredible amount of power in your kicks. Kicking techniques are used for self-defence, sparring and breaking moves. Several parts of the foot are used for performing kicks and for breaking, including the ball of the foot, the base of the heel, the back of the heel, and the footsword (the side of the foot).

Your leg is three times as strong as your arm, and obviously much longer. So it provides a person with a much greater reach. This is why so many of the movements in Taekwon-Do are performed with the legs. If the distance is there for you to be able to kick, then you will soon be able easily to unleash a flurry of fast, powerful kicks before an opponent can close the distance.

1 Remember to keep a certain distance between you and your opponent.

2 Take your rear leg behind your kicking leg as you close in to deliver the kick.

3 Keep your knee high as you prepare to kick.

4 Straighten you leg right out at the moment of impact and strike the target with your heel.

33

## Side Kick – Yop Chagi

The most used kick in Taekwon-Do, since students are taught to shape their body facing sideways onto their opponents, the sidekick is easy to deliver from that angle.

It is usually delivered with the heel of the foot, and the toes pulled back towards the body and slightly lower than the heel. Using the heel, which is the hardest part of the foot, to strike the target makes the side kick an extremely powerful one.

Your body should be in a straight line when the kick is delivered, and your kicking leg locked out straight. The kick is usually made with the leading leg, and is aimed at the middle section of the opponent's body, while your other foot should rotate to face away from your opponent.

( TIP ) When sparring, this is the kick that you use to keep your opponent at bay.

1 *Again, always keep your distance from your opponent.*

2 *Lift your kicking leg as you pivot on the ball of your supporting (rear) leg.*

34

## Turning Kick – Dollyo Chagi

Another frequently used kick in Taekwon-Do, particularly in sparring and self-defence situations, the turning kick is delivered with the ball of the foot, or the instep. It can also be performed by both the front and rear legs.

As you deliver the kick, you need to pivot on the ball of the foot of your supporting leg. This way you can turn into the kick, and so generate power through the technique.

If you are going to be kicking off your front leg, then a little bit of power will be sacrificed for speed, because although the kick can be delivered quicker, it has slightly less power than a kick from the rear leg.

The turning kick is usually aimed at an opponent's head, or the middle section of the body.

( TIP ) *Always remember to pivot on the ball of the foot of your supporting leg. If you don't, you will lose power, technique and possibly strain your leg muscles.*

3 *Make sure that your rear foot is facing away from your opponent as you bring your front leg round in an arc to deliver the kick with the ball of your foot or the instep.*

1 Make sure that there is enough distance between you and your opponent when you begin.

2 Bring your rear leg round, lifting your knee up, as you pivot on the ball of your front foot.

3 Shape the foot of your attacking leg as it comes round and make sure your toes are lower than your heel.

4 Strike your target with the back of your heel as this makes a stronger impact.

35

## Reverse Turning Kick – Bandae Dollyo Chagi

This is the opposite of the turning kick and is used equally well offensively or defensively. It uses the back heel or the palm (sole) of the foot to strike the target and is usually aimed at the high section (the head, jaw, or temple) of an opponent, though it can be directed at their middle section too.

The kick is delivered from the rear leg, while the front leg acts as support. Once again, you should make sure that you pivot on the ball of the foot of your supporting leg, turning your foot 180 degrees so that it faces away from your target. At the same time, the rear leg arcs round in a circular motion, and the back heel of the attacking foot, or the palm of the foot strikes the opponent.

1 Keep your distance from your opponent, who should be doing likewise.

2 Pivot on the ball of your front foot as you raise your kicking leg and position your knee.

3 Shape your kicking foot with your toes pulled back towards you. Your front foot will now be facing away from your opponent.

4 Make sure you deliver this kick with your heel as it will generate more power.

## Back Kick – Dwit Cha Chagi

Arguably the most powerful kick used in Taekwon-Do, the back kick is primarily used for defensive purposes, because you need to turn your back on your opponent for a split second before releasing the strike. The reasoning behind its use for defence only is that it is not wise to come forward and turn your back at the same time.

You use your rear leg and the heel of the foot to deliver a back kick and, as with the side kick, it can generate a lot of power. You pivot on the supporting front leg, between 90 and 180 degrees, while either you bring your rear leg round in a circular direction, or up and out in a straight line. And, as you bring your rear leg round (in whichever fashion you choose), your body should also turn through 180 degrees. Your kicking leg should end up in the same position as it would if you had done a side kick, that is, your leg should be straight as the heel of the foot hits your intended target.

( TIP ) *This kick is best used when someone comes in to attack you.*

1 *Keep a distance between you and your opponent.*

2 *Raise your knee to chest height and shape your foot so that your toes are pulled back towards you.*

## Front Snap Kick – Ap Cha Busigi

Delivered very quickly, the front snap kick uses the ball of the foot to strike an opponent, and the target is usually his or her middle section, that is, the stomach.

You need to be facing your opponent to deliver this kick properly, but you can use either the front or the rear leg. Bring your knee up so that it is level with your waist as your foot snaps out and strikes your target. You then withdraw your leg as quickly as possible back to its starting position.

37

3 *Bring your leg up in to a straight line and strike with the ball of your foot to the face, stomach or groin.*

1 Keep a distance between you and your opponent.

2 Pull your leg in towards you as you shape your foot.

3 Arc your leg round coming in towards your opponent to strike.

4 You can strike with either the back of your heel or the sole of your foot. Usually, the kick would be aimed to the jaw or temple.

## Hooking Kick – Gorro Chagi

Although the hooking kick can be delivered with either the back heel, or the palm (sole) of the foot, it is more powerful if delivered with the back heel. The hooking kick is usually performed as an attacking kick, though it is sometimes used defensively as well.

As you strike with this kick, you should be standing more or less sideways on to your opponent. You use your front leg to kick with and the foot of your rear supporting leg needs to be turned to point between 90 and 180 degrees away from your opponent. Then you arc your kicking leg in a circular motion, coming from the outside in towards to strike your target.

1 *Keeping your distance from your opponent, prepare to pivot on the ball of your front foot.*

2 *As you pivot round on the ball of your front foot, bring your rear leg up and in towards your opponent.*

3 *Make sure that your foot is shaped so that your toes are pulled back towards you and are slightly lower than your heel.*

4 *Strike with your heel and hook your leg round and through the target area.*

39

## Reverse Hooking Kick – Bandae Gorro Chagi

Just as the reverse turning kick is the opposite of the turning kick, so this is the opposite of the hooking kick. It is mainly used as a defensive kick, and is frequently used in sparring.

You use the back of your heel to strike the target area, though as with the hooking kick, the palm (sole) of the foot can also be used.

This kick is performed in nearly the same way as a reverse turning kick, that is with your back leg, but the difference is that, as you arc your leg up and round, the lower part of your leg is pulled (hooked) through the target area just before impact is made. The result is that this reverse hooking kick is delivered faster than a reverse turning kick.

( TIP ) *This kick is best used defensively. An incredible amount of power can be generated through it, but you need to have good balance when you are using this technique. Obviously your balance should be better when you are stationary and using this kick as part of a counterattack.*

# BASIC BLOCKS

Blocks are very important in Taekwon-Do, and they make use of various parts of the body. They are designed to stop an attack and to give you the chance to make a quick counterattack, if needed. The various parts of your feet, arms and hands that you block with are often referred to as blocking 'tools'. The forearms are considered to be the best and are indeed the most commonly used, because they are strong with large muscle groups in them, and can withstand strong blows from opponents.

When blocking you do not actually have to come into physical contact with your opponent's attack. If you can move your body out of the way of an attack, then so much the better because you will still have your forearms, hands, or whatever other blocking tool you might have been using, in a position to be able to hit back or block again if necessary.

Hand positions can vary a great deal when you are blocking – they can be shaped into the knifehand position, as a fist, or open and flat, or in a grasping or hook-like shape to name but a few.

1

1 *Your arm should be bent into a slight 'V'.*

2 *Make sure that your knuckles are shoulder height as you block.*

## Inner Forearm Middle Block – An Bakat Palmok Kaundae Makgi

A commonly used block in Taekwon-Do, the inner forearm middle block is primarily used in self-defence situations. It can come from either side of your body, but is more than likely to come from the front, especially in a self-defence situation, as you should be facing your attacker. You use what is known as the inside part of your forearm, that is the part of your forearm which would be nearest to you if you were standing with your arms relaxed and by your sides.

2

Usually the fist is closed at the moment of impact, but you can also perform this block with your fist shaped as a knifehand (see page 44). As the attacker goes to strike you, bring your arm up and through the centre line of your body and, as you are doing this, rotate your wrist so that your knuckles are facing away from your body. Use the middle part of your forearm to block, and keep your arm relaxed until the final moment of impact, when you should then tense your arm.

( TIP ) *Slightly twist your hips into this block, as this will generate more force.*

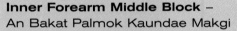

1 *As with the inner forearm block, your arm should be in a slight 'V' shape with your knuckles at shoulder height.*

### Outer Forearm Middle Block – Bakat Palmok Kaundae Makgi

42

Another often used block, the outer forearm middle block is the opposite of the previous block. Again, this block is good to use in self-defence situations, though it is also frequently used as a block when sparring.

It usually comes from the centre of your body, and you need to raise your arm up so that your fist is at chest height and then slightly arc your arm out to the side, rotating your wrist so that your knuckles end up facing you.

You should try to block and make impact with the middle of your outer forearm, that is the part of the forearm furthest away from your body when your arms are relaxed and by your sides.

( TIP ) *As with the inner forearm middle block, you should try slightly to twist your hips into this technique, as it will help you to generate more force into your block.*

2 *Keep your arm bent because doing so creates resistance in the block.*

1 *Turn you wrist, so that you use the bony, outer side of your forearm to block an object being aimed downwards at you.*

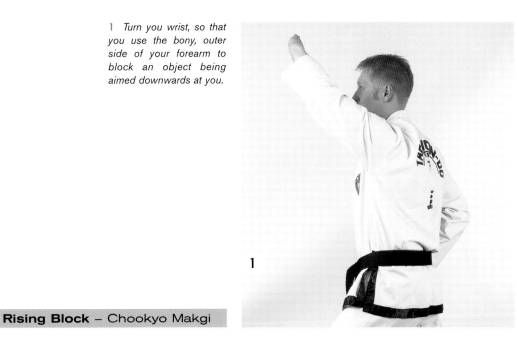

## Rising Block – Chookyo Makgi

The rising block is used to deflect an attacking tool that is coming towards your head, or the high section of your body, and it is usually performed while you are in a walking stance. You use your outer forearm and your hand should be shaped into a fist, which gives you more strength and force, though you can also have your hand in a knifehand shape.

43

As you begin the block, bring your blocking arm up through the centre line of your body, and rotate your wrist and hand so that your knuckles end up facing you. Make sure that you are blocking with the bony, outer edge of your forearm, not the muscular, inner side. Your hand should be 15–25 cm (6–10 inches) away from your forehead, with your arm above your head.

2 *Keep your hand about half a forearm's length away from your head as you block.*

*1 Make sure you tuck your thumb in towards your palm as you perform this block.*

## Knifehand Block – Sonkal Makgi

This block can be performed with both the outer and inner parts of the forearm. A knifehand middle block would be performed in exactly the same way as an outer forearm middle block, while a knifehand rising block is performed in exactly the same way as a normal rising block.

( TIP ) *All knifehand blocks work well, but they do not have as much resistance in them as a block where your hand is shaped into a fist.*

*2 As with the rising block on the previous page, keep your hand about half a forearm's length away from your head.*

*1 Make sure that your rear arm and hand are protecting your solar plexus.*

**1**

## Knifehand Guarding Block – Sonkal Daebi Makgi

Used in a lot of the patterns in Taekwon-Do, the knifehand guarding block is usually performed in 'L' stance as you face sideways on to your attacker. Your leading arm is held out in front of you (as you look at it from the side, the arm should look as if it is in a 'V'), with your hand held in the knifehand position, palm facing downwards, and fingertips at shoulder height.

The elbow of your rear arm should be roughly on your hip, though a little way away from it, and your rear hand should also be shaped into a knifehand, and again held just in front of your solar plexus (abdomen). From here, the rear hand can easily protect the solar plexus, or can be used to make a forceful counterattack, as you can deliver a punch from the hip area.

( TIP ) *Always tuck your thumbs in when performing knifehand blocks or techniques, as it's easy to catch them on an opponent's attack or clothing.*

45

**2**

*2 Keep your front arm bent into a slight 'V' and the fingertips of your hand at shoulder height.*

1 *It is possible to counterattack with a punch at the same time as you use this block.*

2 *Your fists should be in a line as you look down at them.*

46

## Forearm Guarding Block – Palmok Daebi Makgi

Although it is performed in the same way as the knifehand guarding block, your hands should be shaped into fists. Again, the forearm guarding block is usually performed in 'L' stance, and is a stronger block than the knifehand guarding block.

With your rear arm already shaped into a fist, and travelling from the hip, it is easy to counterattack quickly with a reverse punch, if the block is successful. It's also easy for you to counterattack with your leading arm once you have absorbed or deflected the oncoming attack.

1 *Bring your blocking arm up to just above your lower stomach.*

2 *Angle your elbow out to the side as you turn your hand over so that the palm is facing downwards.*

## Downward Block – Naeryo Makgi

A downward block is usually performed with the palm of the hand, though it can also be performed with the inner or outer forearm, with your hand shaped as a fist or a knifehand. It is a good block for you to be able to bring down your attacker's kick or punch, as the block is designed to come down on top of whichever attack your opponent is throwing at you.

You perform the block in a circular motion with whichever blocking tool you are applying.

( TIP ) *Try to keep your elbow at an angle of 45 degrees as you perform this block.*

47

3 *Push down with your palm as you block and angle your elbow out to approximately 45 degrees.*

*Try not to lean forwards too much in this stance.*

These intermediate stances are slightly more advanced than the basic ones in the chapter on page 20 because you use your body to a greater degree and focus on your balance more. Some of the stances featured also allow you to move more quickly from a defensive to an attacking position.

# INTERMEDIATE STANCES

## 'X' Stance – Kyocha Sogi

This stance is not used very often, but features in several patterns and is useful for when you want to move quickly into another stance or technique. Once in the 'X' stance, it is easy to move and attack to the front or to the side. With your legs crossed over one another and slightly bent, you put your front foot flat on the floor and stand on the ball of your rear foot. Your weight is placed on your front foot, and you should make sure that that foot is firmly planted on the floor.

( TIP ) *Try to keep your back straight because it's easy to lose your balance if you lean over your feet too much.*

*Your weight should be on your front foot, as you only use the ball of your rear foot to maintain your balance.*

1 *The majority of your weight will be placed on your rear foot in this stance. The heel of your rear foot should be just behind the heel of your front foot.*

2 *Your rear foot should also be bent slightly outwards.*

49

## Rear Foot Stance – Dwitbal Sogi

The rear foot stance is more of a defensive stance than an attacking one.

Your feet should be one shoulder width apart, as you measure from the outer edges of your feet. Your rear leg should be bent slightly inwards, with the foot planted firmly on the floor, while your front leg should be bent so that the ball of the foot is touching the ground. The majority of your weight should be on your rear foot.

In this stance, it is quite easy for you to kick off the front leg, either defensively or offensively, and to move your weight either forwards or backwards quite swiftly.

*1 Distribute your weight evenly between both legs.*

Your feet should be roughly one-and-a-half shoulder widths apart with one leg in front of the other, and your legs should bend at the knees, as in the sitting stance. Your leading leg should face your opponent, while your rear leg faces roughly 90 degrees to the side.

## Fixed Stance – Gojung Sogi

A strong stance which is used for both attack and defence, where your weight is distributed equally on both legs.

*2 Bend your knees as you would in sitting stance. Don't lock your front leg out straight.*

*1 Remember to keep your head up and your back straight to maintain your balance.*

*2 Shape your front foot so that it is pulled up and tucked in by the side of your knee.*

51

## Bending Stance – Goburyo Sogi

Primarily a defensive stance, you can execute either a side kick, or a back kick quite easily from bending stance.

For this stance you balance on your supporting leg, which should be bent at the knee so that your knee comes over your foot. Your other leg is also bent at the knee and raised so that the foot is at an angle, with the toes bent upwards, and held by the side of the knee on your supporting leg.

1   *Place more weight on your rear foot in the vertical stance rather than on the front.*

2   *Turn your feet inwards slightly – about 15 degrees from their starting points – and straighten your legs.*

52

## Vertical Stance – Soojik Sogi

The most natural of all the stances in Taekwon-Do, the vertical stance is one in which you find yourself standing almost everyday.

Both your legs should be straight, with one slightly in front of the other so that your feet are about one-shoulder width apart. Your front foot faces forwards, and your rear foot to the side, while both feet are turned inwards about 15 degrees. Your weight should be distributed so that about 60 per cent of it is over the rear leg, and 40 per cent on the front.

1 *Keep your body in a straight line, making sure your posture is good.*

2 *Your feet should be together and your toes should be touching.*

## Close Stance – Moa Sogi

Usually used when you are going from one stance to another, close stance is also used as the initial stance for several patterns, and though normally performed towards the front, it can sometimes be performed to the side.

Your feet should be together, but your arms can be held in a variety of positions. The most common is to hold them out in front, with the elbows tucked into your side, and your hands (shaped as fists) held slightly lower than the elbow joint.

*1 Keep your feet about one and a half shoulder widths apart.*

## Crouched Stance – Oguryo Sogi

Quite a strong stance, the crouched stance is often used when sparring.

Your knees need to be pushed inwards, slightly towards each other, and your feet need to be roughly one-and-a-half shoulder widths apart, with the big toe of your rear foot in a horizontal line with the back heel of your front foot. Your legs are quite strong in this stance because they are tensed as you bend your knees inwards, but your knees can be vulnerable to an attack from the side.

*2 Push your knees inwards slightly as you sit down into this stance.*

*1 Angle your feet outwards to roughly 45 degrees as you assume this stance. Your legs should be locked out straight.*

## Ready Stance – Chunbi Sogi

You usually take up the ready stance before you begin to perform a pattern or any other movement. Your feet should be at a 45-degree angle, as you stand with your legs slightly apart. Your hands should be in a fist shape, and you should let your arms drop by your side, with your elbows slightly bent.

*2 Bend your arms slightly and keep your hands in a fist shape.*

1 *Keep your face and chin guarded as you perform the uppercut punch because it is usually thrown at close quarters, so you need to protect yourself.*

1

# INTERMEDIATE PUNCHES AND HAND STRIKES

The hand strikes and punches shown here use various different parts of the hand to strike your opponent and they also include elbow strikes which you can perform in three different ways.

## Uppercut Punch – Ollyo Jurugi

A very powerful punch which is best used at short range, the uppercut punch is a very effective self-defence technique. But it is not commonly used when sparring, because of the distance involved when sparring in Taekwon-Do, as so many kicks are being thrown.

2

This punch is designed to hit your attacker on the chin, and should travel up through the centre line of your body. Your hand should be shaped into a fist, and your knuckles should be facing away from your body. You should try to connect with the first two knuckles, and if you are able to dip your body a little and bend your knees before you stand up straight, then you will be able to put more force into the punch. You can throw this punch either when your hands are on your chest, or when they are held low down.

2 *Try to strike with the first two knuckles of your hand.*

( TIP ) *Make sure that you throw this punch through the middle of your opponent's guard.*

1  *Strike with the lower part of your hand.*

2  *Keep your hand relatively flat and taut at the moment of impact.*

## Palm Strike – Sonbadak Terrigi

This can be a devastating self-defence strike. Primarily a palm strike is aimed at the nose, though a palm strike to the eardrum or the temple can be nearly as effective.

Your hand is open as you perform this strike, with your fingers together and pulled slightly back as you strike so as not to damage them. The aim is to hit your attacker with the lower two muscles (just below your thumb and above your wrist) of your palm; however the centre of the palm to a nose is also effective.

If you try to strike the temple or an eardrum, then you must try to use the muscles as mentioned.

Palm strikes are not permitted when you are sparring in Taekwon-Do.

1

*1  Strike with the muscle running from the base of your little finger to the wrist and make sure that your knuckles are facing away from you when you hit your target.*

## Inner Knifehand Strike – Sonkal Terrigi

Once again, inner knifehand strikes are better used as self-defence techniques rather than for sparring. They are most commonly aimed at an attacker's neck, either to the side or to the front.

58

In this instance, that is, when performing knifehand strikes inwards, the striking part of your hand is the muscle that runs from the base of the little finger to the ball joint of the wrist. This is quite a fleshy part of the hand, and it will not hurt you when you hit your target.

Your knuckles should be facing away from your body as you strike your opponent. If your hands are by your side when you go to strike, make sure that your knuckles are facing you and then rotate your wrist and hand so that the knuckles face away from you as you hit the target area. You should bring your arm up in an arcing motion travelling inwards.

( TIP ) *Twist your hips into the technique for additional power.*

2

*2  Keep your hand shaped and your arm slightly bent as you make impact with your target.*

1 *Use the side of your index finger to make the strike and tuck your thumb underneath as far as possible.*

## Outer Knifehand Strike – Bakat Sonkal Terrigi

Obviously this is the opposite of the inner knifehand strike. With this technique, you have to take your hand from the inside outwards and back in again to the intended target, so it arcs round before it actually strikes.

You use the top of your index finger to the knuckle at the bottom of it with which to attack, but try mainly to use the knuckle, which should be facing you as you start and finish this strike.

( TIP ) *This technique is effective in sparring when someone has attacked and missed you and they are travelling past you. It is easy from here to deliver an outer knifehand strike quickly to their head.*

2 *Make sure that the hand with which you strike is kept flat and use your free arm to guard your face and body.*

59

1 *Keep your arm straight and in line with your shoulder as you bring it across your chest.*

### Front Elbow Strike – Ap Palkop Terrigi

60

There are various elbow strikes (*Palkop Terrigi*) which you will learn to perform as you progress through your training. They are excellent self-defence techniques because they are extremely powerful and effective at close range, but they are not permitted in sparring as they are too dangerous.

The front elbow strike is probably the most common. Not surprisingly, you hit your target with the front (lower) part of your elbow. As your hands are at your sides, bring the hand of the arm you are using up and across your chest, making sure that it finishes at the same height as your opposite shoulder and that your forearm is in a horizontal line. The elbow itself should come up in a circular motion. The best target to hit with a front elbow strike is the nose.

2 *Strike your opponent with the front part of your elbow, which is just below the joint itself, and not the tip.*

An elbow strike should be used at very close range, where it is not possible to kick and difficult to punch. In this position, it is hard for your attacker to see this technique coming.

( TIP ) *Take care not to catch the target with the tip of your elbow, as this could cause you injury.*

*1 Strike your target with the back part of your elbow, that is just above the joint, rather than the tip.*

## Side Elbow Strike – Yop Palkop Terrigi

Another very effective technique to use in a self-defence situation, this time you strike with the back (higher) part of the elbow and, as with the front elbow strike, the forearm is kept in a horizontal position from start to finish, although the side elbow strike is performed in a linear motion as opposed to a circular motion.

As you make the strike, you have to bring your arm slightly in the opposite direction to the side you wish to hit, before bringing your arm up and out into the horizontal shape as the back of your elbow connects with the target area.

*2 Make sure that your hands are shaped as fists so that your arms are tensed and strong when you strike.*

*1 Bend you arm and bring it up quickly so that the front part of your elbow strikes your opponent.*

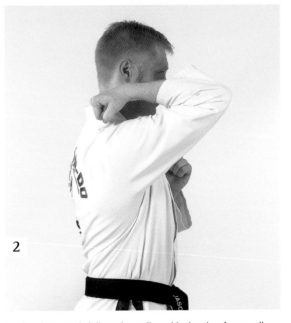

1

## Upper Elbow Strike –
Wi Palkop Terrigi

Of all the elbow strikes, the upper elbow strike is the most powerful and effective.

As with the front elbow strike, you use the front (lower) part of the elbow to strike with but it is performed in a linear motion.

If you are standing, then the target area for this strike is usually under your attacker's chin. Stand with your hands by your sides and shape the hand of the arm you are hitting with into a fist. Then pull it up quickly towards your shoulder. As you do this, your elbow will be travelling upwards, and from here you need to aim it to the underside of your opponent's chin as mentioned. If you are able to, try to bend your knees slightly and dip your body and then stand up as you strike. This adds extra body weight and power to your strike.

( TIP ) *Try to aim your elbow between your attacker's arms.*

2

*2 Don't try and deliver the strike with the tip of your elbow. You should aim for your attacker's chin.*

1 *Strike your target with the first two knuckles of your fist.*

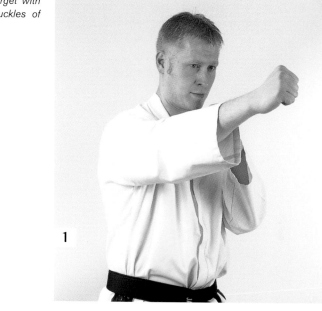

## Back Fist – Dung Joomuk

A very quick technique which you can use in a self-defence situation or in sparring, the back fist can be classed as a punch.

Your hand is shaped into a fist, while your knuckles face away from your body as you prepare to use this technique, and you use the first two knuckles to strike your target. When you are ready, you snap your fist towards the target, and then immediately pull it back.

2 *Keep up your guard before and after you deliver this punch.*

*1  Raise your arm while
you are shaping your hand
into a fist.*

*2  Bring your fist down
onto your target and strike
with the underside.*

1

2

## Hammer Fist Strike – Yop Joomuk

Sometimes called the side fist, the hammer fist is similar to the back fist, the difference being that you use the bottom of your fist to strike your intended target.

You shape your hand into a fist, and position it vertically so that your knuckles are facing away from your body. You strike with the muscle that runs from the bottom of the little finger to the ball of the wrist, as in the inner knifehand strike.

The hammer fist strike is usually used in a downwards motion onto an opponent's nose, shoulder, chest or the top of the head, though it can be effective to use when striking to the side.

1 *Either step back or pull your shoulder back as your form a fist.*

2 *Strike with the first two knuckles of your hand and maintain eye contact with your opponent since this punch can take your target by surprise if it is delivered low.*

## Straight-line Punch –
## Sun Jurugi

A punch that is best used in self-defence rather than sparring (because it works best at close range and obviously you don't get many opportunities like that in sparring), the straight-line punch requires you to take a slight step backwards or to pull your shoulder back to chamber the punch just as almost all the other punches do.

You should hold your fist in a vertical position, and be facing your opponent as you strike him or her. From a standing position, you bring your hand up and onto the target area in a linear motion. Try to hit your target with the first two knuckles on your fist.

The target area for this punch is usually the centre of the chest, or the solar plexus, but the nose and the chin are also good targets.

( TIP ) *Twist you hips into the punch as you deliver it.*

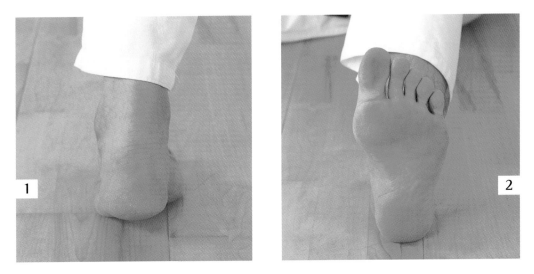

# INTERMEDIATE KICKS

Building on what you learnt in the Basic Kicks chapter, you will find that these kicks are slightly more difficult to perform. There are various attacking and defensive kicks included, some of which are used for blocking other kicks. Plus there are also some jumping kicks. All the kicks are used quite frequently in Taekwon-Do, but your instructor will not teach them to you until he or she is happy that you are familiar with the basics. Firstly, though, there is a review of the different parts of the foot that are used in the various kicks.

1 *The back heel is used for delivering kicks such as the reverse hooking kick (see page 39), the axe kick (see page 68) and the reverse turning kick (see page 35).*

2 *The ball of the foot is used for kicks like the front snap kick (see page 37) and the turning kick (see page 34).*

3 *The footsword (side of the foot) can be used for side kicks (eg the side checking kick on page 70) and crescent kicks, such as that on page 73.*

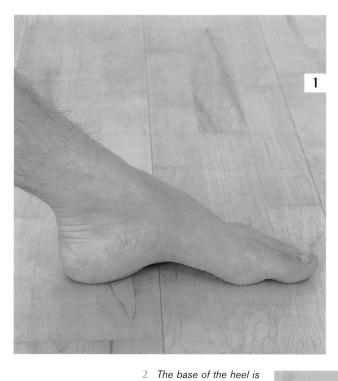

**1** *The instep is used for delivering kicks such as the outer sweep kick (see page 79).*

**2** *The base of the heel is used for striking with kicks such as the side kick (see page 33) and the back kick (see page 36).*

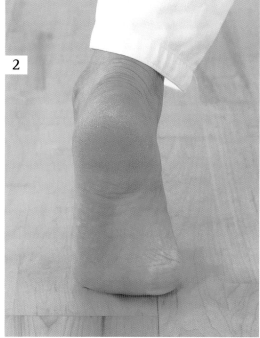

1 *You and your opponent should take up your stances in readiness to attack or defend.*

2 *The axe kick is performed by swinging your leg upwards from the outside of your body inwards.*

3 *You should raise your kicking leg as high as possible as you deliver this kick with the back of your heel.*

4 *Keeping your kicking leg straight, bring it down onto your opponent's shoulder.*

## Axe Kick – Naero Chagi

The axe kick is used quite often in sparring because it can be used both offensively and defensively to great effect. It is designed to hit either your opponent's collarbone, or to be brought down onto your opponent's nose.

You use either the back part of your heel, or the palm (sole) of your foot. As you kick, you need to pull your leg up as high as possible towards your shoulder, and then chop it straight back down onto your target. Your leg must be kept locked out and straight throughout the whole technique.

( TIP ) *Lean your body backwards as you connect with this kick.*

1  *Again, assume a stance which allows you the opportunity to attack or defend accordingly.*

2  *Your opponent aims a kick at you.*

## Front Checking Kick –
## Ap Cha Mum Chagi

A self-defence kick, the front checking kick is not permitted in sparring, because it can cause serious injury. It is used either to stop a kick that is being thrown against you, or to disable somebody, and usually performed from a forward facing position, so that when your attacker goes to raise their leg, you will be able to stamp down on their shin or kneecap.

You attack with your instep. As you strike, you should angle your foot out to the side at approximately 15 degrees.

69

3  *The front checking kick is performed using the instep, which you aim just above your opponent's foot to ward off his kick.*

1  *You and your opponent prepare to attack or defend as necessary.*

## Side Checking Kick – Yop Cha Mum Chagi

A variation on the front checking kick, the side checking kick would be used (not surprisingly!) if you were sideways on to your opponent. As with the front checking kick, the side checking kick is an effective self-defence technique and the target areas are again the kneecap or the shinbone.

From this position, you use the footsword (the outer edge) of your foot. As you perform this kick, lean your body backwards slightly, so you are take your upper body out of reach of an attack.

( TIP ) *This kick is an effective counter against a high attack.*

2  *Another way of countering a kick (here coming from the attacker on the right) is to turn sideways and kick using your footsword (the side of your foot).*

1 The opponents prepare to attack.

2 To perform the jump side kick you should turn sideways and, as you jump, prepare to aim a side kick at your opponent's chest while tucking your other leg underneath your body.

## Jump Side Kick – Twigi Yop Chagi

The jump side kick is a technique which is usually used as for sparring rather than self-defence.

As with the side kick, you use your heel to strike the target. When you start to jump, you should bend your knees slightly, and then push yourself up in a straight line, remembering to keep your head up, and your back straight. As you do this, tuck your rear leg – the leg that you are not kicking with – under your body, while you extend your kicking leg in a straight line at the moment when your body is at its highest point of the jump. On finishing your kick, quickly retract your kicking leg and drop your rear leg to prepare for your landing.

( TIP ) Remember to pull your toes back towards your body, and strike with the heel.

71

3 The side kick is delivered with the heel as your leg shoots out towards your opponent, while you bring your other leg up towards your body.

1   *The opponents prepare to confront each other.*

2   *The jump back kick is done by jumping up and round 180° so that you will have your back to your opponent.*

3   *Turning your face towards your opponent, you kick out with the base of your heel.*

4   *You should deliver the back kick to your opponent's chest.*

## Jump Back Kick – Twigi Dwit Cha Chagi

A very powerful kick to use, the jump back kick is more suited to sparring than self-defence. As with the back kick, you will be using the base of your heel to strike your opponent, which means you can put a lot of power into this kick. Like the jump side kick, you must remember to keep your head up and your back straight as you jump.

The kick comes off your rear leg, so as you jump, you spin your body around 180 degrees towards your opponent for a split second, so that you are facing him or her when you hit them. Try to tuck the leg you are not kicking with under your body as you kick.

TIP   *Take care not to lean your upper body too far backwards as you execute this kick. It's easy to do and affects your technique, balance, and the power of the kick.*

1  Again, the opponents both take up a walking stance.

2  Bring your leg up in an arc from the outside inwards towards your opponent.

3  Straighten your leg out as you swing it in towards your opponent's head.

4  You should aim to hit your opponent with the sole of your foot, bringing your leg through the arc to the opposite side of your body.

73

## Crescent Kick – Bandal Chagi

Used in both sparring and self-defence, the crescent kick is primarily used to block, and the part of the foot used is the sole of the foot. With this kick, you can strike your opponent's hand, leg, elbow or forearm.

This kick is usually performed from a forwards facing position using the sole of the foot. Your leg should be bent at the knee, to allow for quick movement of the lower leg, as you arc it up from an outward to an inward position. Your foot should be turned in towards you, so that the sole is in a vertical position.

1   The opponents assume their stances, ready to attack or defend.

2   Bring your leg up in an arc, with your knee slightly bent, this time moving from the inside outwards.

3   Straighten your leg out as it moves through the arc and pivot on the ball of your other foot.

4   Deliver the kick to your opponent's head with your footsword and take your leg down and outwards.

### Reverse Crescent Kick – Bandae Bandal Chagi

The reverse crescent kick is not really used as a self-defence kick but more as a counterattacking sparring technique. With the reverse crescent kick, you strike your opponent with the footsword (outer edge) of your foot, and the kick comes from your rear leg.

At the beginning of the move, you will need to pivot between 270 and 360 degrees on the ball of the foot of your front leg and while you are pivoting on your front leg, you whip your rear leg round in an arc from an outward to an inward position and your footsword should then strike your target with your leg finishing in front of your body.

1 *The opponents take up a stance, ready to attack or defend.*

2 *Bring your rear leg up and outwards.*

3 *Then twist your bent leg back inwards towards your opponent's thigh.*

4 *Aim to kick the inside of your opponent's thigh with the ball of your foot.*

75

## Twisting Kick – Bituro Chagi

This kick is designed to work as a low level kick, but it can also be aimed at your opponent's top section. The best target area, though, is the inside of your attacker's thigh, or their kneecap, but other targets include the stomach (from the middle section) and the jaw.

You use the ball of your foot and, as you kick, you should pull your toes back and out of the way. Your foot should also be turned in, at an angle of about 15 degrees, towards the target area, so that it is in a vertical position.

1   The opponents face up to each other.

2   In this instance the rear leg is brought up to administer the kick.

3   Raise your leg to chest level and shape your foot.

4   Place the sole of your foot into your opponent's chest.

5   Release the kick by pushing your opponent backwards.

## Front Push Kick – Ap Cha Milgi

A variation on the front snap kick, the front push kick can come either from the back or the front leg and is done as you travel forwards.

For this kick, you use the sole of your foot to strike your opponent and, as you start to kick, you should pull the knee of your kicking leg up towards your chest to prime the kick before you release it. You release the kick by pushing your kicking leg forwards, so that the sole of your foot lands on and pushes through the intended target. The momentum of the kick helps to push your target away, whereas the front snap kick will hit the target but not push it away.

( TIP ) Remember to bring your knee up to a high position on your chest.

1 You will need to face your opponent for this kick.

2 Grasp the back of your opponent's head with both hands.

## Knee Kick – Moorup Chagi

One of the most effective self-defence kicks that you can learn (it is not permitted in sparring), the knee kick is best used when you are at very close range to your attacker, so it is also possible to grab him or her as you deliver it. There are several target areas that you can aim for, the most common being the groin, the ribs and the stomach or, if you can grab your attacker and pull them downwards, the face.

The knee kick is delivered with the top part of the knee, and all you need to do is raise your knee up to the target area. This is easy to do if you are aiming at the groin, but if you are aiming for somewhere else, you will probably need to grab your opponent to be able to deliver the kick effectively.

3 Pull your opponent's head down, while keeping your fingers locked together.

4 Bring your leg up to meet your opponent's head and strike his nose with your knee.

1  *Each opponent takes up a stance, ready to attack or defend.*

2  *Bring your rear leg round in a sweeping motion, keeping it down, just above floor level.*

## Inner Sweep Kick – An Suroh Chagi

The inner sweep kick is a very effective technique for taking your opponent down to the floor. It is useful for self-defence purposes and is sometimes permitted when sparring, and can be used in both an attacking or a defensive mode.

Using the inner side of the sole (underneath the arch) of your foot, the idea behind this kick is that you try and sweep aside your opponent's ankle from the inside, thus causing them to lose their balance and hopefully fall over.

( TIP )  *The inner sweep kick is very effective when used at a very close range. It is also good as a follow-up technique after an initial close range strike.*

3  *Deliver a strike with your instep to your opponent's ankle.*

4  *After you have made contact keep your foot moving through the target area.*

1 Once more, the opponents have taken up a stance, ready to attack or defend.

2 Keeping your foot low, bring your foot round to the outside of your opponent's ankle.

## Outer Sweep Kick – Bakat Suroh Chagi

The reverse of the inner sweep kick, the outer sweep kick is designed to target the outside of your attacker's ankle. This kick is very effective if your opponent has committed him or herself to a technique which you have blocked and it is easier to use from a longer range than the inner sweep kick.

As with the inner sweep kick, you use the side of the sole of your foot for your attacking tool.

3 Use your instep to deliver the kick as your foot comes round.

4 Keep your foot moving through the kick, so forcing your opponent's leg off the ground to make him lose balance.

1   *Your opponent may grab your wrist.*

2   *Let your opponent maintain his grip while you bring your knee up ready to kick.*

## Front Rising Kick – Ap Cha Olligi

Primarily used as a self-defence technique, rather than for sparring, the front rising kick is best applied from a walking stance. It is usually aimed underneath your attacker's forearm as they punch in order to deflect the punch and make it rise up and away from you.

You use the ball of your foot to strike with, and your toes should be pulled back towards your body, to avoid catching them on, or kicking your opponent.

3   *Using the ball of your foot, deliver a kick to your opponent's forearm.*

4   *This rising kick should then make your opponent release his grasp.*

1  *A waving kick can fend off an attack from the side.*

2  *In this case, your opponent (on the right) is beginning a low kick to your foot or ankle.*

## Waving Kick – Doro Chagi

The waving kick is a self-defence kick and usually performed from a sitting stance, or when you are standing sideways on to your attacker. It is a good technique to use against someone who has tried to kick your ankle and sweep you off balance. It is also good for blocking a kick to your groin!

With this kick, you strike your attacker with your footsword, aiming for his or ankle. As your attacker goes to kick you, you should withdraw the leg which your attacker is aiming at and pull the sole of your foot up towards your groin, from where you can quickly execute the waving kick down towards your opponent's ankle.

3  *As your opponent tries to deliver his kick, bring your foot up and out of the way.*

4  *Take your foot back down immediately and kick with your footsword at your opponent's foot or ankle.*

The intermediate blocks described in this chapter are all used quite frequently, especially in the *tuls* or patterns. They are slightly more intricate than the basic blocks and include several 'double blocks', which is the performing of two blocks against two different attacks.

1  *Bring your arms up and across your face to form an 'X'.*

1

# INTERMEDIATE BLOCKS

## X-Fist Rising Block –
### Kyocha Chookyo Makgi

A good block to use in a walking stance, the X-fist rising block is designed for use against an object or attack coming down towards your head. The idea of this block is that you catch the attacking arm, leg, or object between your fists and, as your fists are held above your head with your arms outstretched, the attack should not be able to reach you.

Both your hands should be shaped into fists, with the knuckles facing inwards towards each other and your right forearm resting on top of your left forearm, just below the wrist.

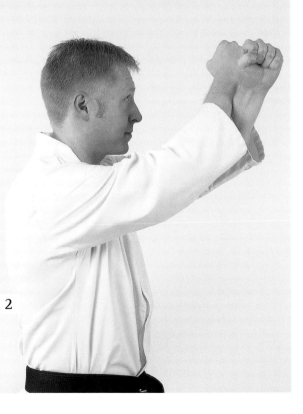

2  *Shape your hands into fists, with the knuckles facing each other, and keep your arms away from your head so that they will absorb the impact of an attack.*

2

**1**

1  *Cross your right forearm over your left to make an 'X' and form your hands into fists.*

2  *To block the kick coming towards you, bring your arms downwards and hold them slightly in front of your groin. Make sure that your hands are turned so that your knuckles are facing each other,*

## X-Fist Downward Block –
Kyocha Naeryo Makgi

Performed in a slightly different way to the X-fist rising block, but obviously, as the name implies, aimed downwards, this block is good for defending against any sort of rising kick being aimed at your groin area.

It is unlike the rising block in that whereas your hands go all the way up in an X-fist rising block in this block they do not go all the way down. Your right forearm should rest on your left forearm (just under the wrist) with your hands turned over slightly so that the knuckles are facing each other. Then, as with the X-fist rising block, you catch the opponent's kick between your fists and force it downwards, so you finish with your hands at roughly the same height as your groin.

**2**

1 *Shape your leading arm in a slight 'V' and form your hands into fists.*

1

### Double Forearm Block –
Doo Palmok Makgi

The double forearm block is good for preventing an attack which is coming from your side or your front.

You use the inner forearm of your leading arm to block, and your hand, which should be at the same height as your shoulder, is shaped into a fist with the knuckles facing away from your body. Extend your arm halfway out, so your elbow joint bends in a 'V' shape. Your rear arm should be shaped as your lead arm, but the fist should be placed on the inside of the elbow of your blocking arm.

( TIP ) *Always make sure that your body is half turned towards your opponent.*

2

2 *The knuckles of your leading hand should be at shoulder height and your rear arm should be shaped as the leading one with the fist positioned on the side of your blocking arm.*

*1 Bring your blocking arm up to shoulder height. Keep your other arm up in a guarding position.*

1

## Pushing Block – Miro Makgi

A fairly simple block which is used for pushing your opponent off balance, the pushing block can be used from a variety of stances, though mainly from a sitting, fixed, or walking stance. You can aim for several target areas, including the top of your opponent's shoulder, the biceps, or the forearm.

You use your palm to block and it is very simple to do.

85

( TIP ) *Always remember to pull your fingers back towards your body, and out of the way as you perform this technique.*

2

*2 Strike with the lower part of your palm, preferably the muscle group at the base, although you can use the whole of your arm depending on the size of your target area.*

*1  Arc your hand outwards towards your target.*

1

## Palm Hooking Block – Sonbadak Gorro Makgi

A block which is used to grab as well as to deflect an attack, the palm hooking block can be used to pull an opponent off balance, if you have blocked their punch.

Using the palm of your hand to block with, you would normally start this block by resting your blocking hand upside down, with the knuckles back to back, on your other hand. From here, turn your blocking hand over so that the knuckles are facing you and your hand position is nearly vertical. Once you have blocked with your palm, it is easy to grab your opponent with the same hand and then pull him or her forwards. Also, note that the block will travel from your inside outwards.

( TIP ) *If you are going to grab your attacker after you have blocked, make sure that you are in a reverse walking stance (see page 21). If you try to grab your opponent and fail, and you have the same leg and arm forward on the same side, there is not much stability on your opposite side, and it is easy to lose, or be pushed off, balance.*

2

*2  The palm of your blocking hand will be turned towards your target so that you can easily grab your opponent and pull him or her towards you.*

86

1 Position your front arm as for an outer forearm middle block and the rear arm as for a rising block. This block allows you to protect yourself against a high attack or one to your mid section.

## Twin Forearm Block – Sang Palmok Makgi

A double block which is designed to deflect an attack from the side and the front at the same time, the twin forearm block can be applied in nearly every stance, but it is best in 'L'.

You shape your front arm into an outer forearm middle block (see page 42) and your rear arm into a rising block (see page 43), with both sets of knuckles facing your body. Your fists should twist round as you make the block.

2 The knuckles of both hands should be facing your body.

1 *Bring your arms across your body and form your hands into fists. The top arm will rest on the bottom one.*

2 *Make sure the outer edge of the forearm takes the impact of the attack, which will usually be coming up towards your front.*

## Checking Block – Mumchau Makgi

A block which is usually used to block kicks, the checking block is normally executed with your forearms.

Your hands should be formed into fists (though you could choose a knifehand instead) and crossed to make a slight 'X', and held roughly at chest height, because this block is almost always employed against a kick aimed at your mid section.

You block using your forearms.

1  *The hand you use to block will come from your side while your other hand may guard your top section.*

2  *As you bring your hand up, turn it over so that the palm is facing upwards.*

## Palm Upward Block –
Sonbadak Ollyo Makgi

Used to deflect your opponent's attack upwards, as you perform the palm upward block, you need to make sure that your hand moves in a circular motion as it comes from your hip and travels upwards to meet your opponent's punch or kick. Do not raise this block higher than your own solar plexus.

3  *As your hand comes up, bring it inwards to catch your opponent's punch or kick that is aimed at your mid section and push it up and out of the way.*

# SPARRING

Sparring and the sporting element of Taekwon-Do form a large part of a student's training and sparring practice is done in most lessons, as it is a chance for a student to develop fighting techniques against others. And practice allows students to measure how effective certain techniques are for them, which techniques are working and which need more work. Regular sparring also helps to improve a student's fitness level and helps him or her to gain confidence, because a positive mental attitude is invaluable when it comes to training and demonstrating one's skills in gradings and competitions.

Sparring means only coming into semi-contact with your opponent. This way both of you have the chance to show skill, speed and technique without each bout degenerating into an untidy and unskilful brawl. The competitive side of Taekwon-Do is now very big and a lot of tournaments and championships are held on a regular basis around the country and internationally by various organisations.

In most competitions, sparring bouts last for two minutes, in which the sparring is 'continuous'. This means that when a technique scores a point the bout keeps going, unlike points sparring, where after the scoring of a point the bout is stopped and then restarted again.

When students spar in class, safety is obviously a concern for any instructor, and so it is usual to wear protective sparring equipment. This consists of a headguard, footpads, sparring gloves, a gum shield, a groin guard and shin protectors (see page 13). The rules of sparring in Taekwon-Do state that all blows must be above the waist, and to the front of the body or to the head. The back of your sparring partner's body and below his or her waist are not target areas. Any kicks and punches may be used in sparring, except techniques which involve elbows and knees.

In this chapter, you will find various basic sparring techniques and combinations which a new student is likely to learn.

1  *Sparring partners take up preparatory fighting stances.*

2  *As the attacker (left) starts to deliver a turning kick, you can pivot on your leading leg and bring up your back leg in order to counter with a back kick.*

## Back Kick to a Turning Kick

In this example, the attacker is performing a turning kick, and the defender is performing a back kick to counter the attack.

The back kick is performed in a linear motion, and the body is turned away from the attacker's kick, whereas the turning kick is performed in a circular motion, so it takes slightly longer than the back kick to perform. The back kick should land on the attacker's chest or stomach area.

3  *The back kick is quickly delivered in a linear motion to the attacker's mid section. The turning kick is deflected because it takes longer to deliver.*

1 *The opponents take up stances ready to fight.*

## Turning Kick to a Side Kick

Here the turning kick is used to defend against a side kick.

Note that the defender moves to the side to avoid the side kick, as he performs the turning kick. The turning kick should land on the attacker's stomach.

2 *The attacker (right) brings his leg up ready to deliver a side kick. As he does so the defender moves to the side.*

3 *The defender then quickly counterattacks with a turning kick before the attacker delivers his side kick.*

1 *The opponents face each other ready to spar.*

## Front Kick to a Turning Kick

This time you can see a front kick used against a turning kick. As the turning kick involves a circular motion, it is slower to perform than the front kick, which is a linear move.

The front kick can be aimed towards the attacker's chest, stomach or face.

93

2 *When the attacker (left) begins to bring his leg round to perform a turning kick, the defender brings his knee up in preparation for delivering a front kick.*

3 *Before the attacker can finish delivering his turning kick, the defender has executed his front kick, snapping his leg up to strike the attacker's chest.*

1 *The sparring partners prepare to begin.*

2 *The attacker (left) begins to deliver a side kick and, as he does so, the defender spins round on his back leg.*

## Back Kick to a Side Kick

A common defence against a side kick is the back kick. The reason for this is that it turns the defender's body away from the side kick and offers an opportunity to kick the attacker when the defender completes his or her turn.

The back kick should be aimed at the attacker's stomach or chest, though the higher it is, the less power it has.

3 *Before the attacker's side kick can reach the defender, the defender has released a back kick to the attacker's chest.*

1  The sparring partners square up to each other.

2  As the attacker (right) brings his knee up and round to deliver a turning kick, the defender lifts his right leg up high.

3  As the attacker's turning kick comes round, the defender moves his body away and prepares to bring his leg down in an axe kick.

4  The defender delivers the axe kick to the attacker's chest.

## Axe kick to a Turning Kick

An axe kick is quite a common kick to use against a turning kick. Here we see the axe kick being delivered before the attacker's turning kick can land on the defender. The axe kick should be aimed at the attacker's nose, chest or shoulder.

1   The sparring partners face each other.

2   When the attacker (right) moves in to deliver a punch, the defender leans back and brings his knee up for a side kick.

3   Before the punch can be delivered, the defender has struck with a side kick.

## Side Kick to a Punch

Here we have a simple technique whereby the defender uses his leg reach to perform a side kick to counter his attacker's punch. Obviously, the attacker will not be able to deliver his punch against this side kick.

## Turning Kick to a Punch

In this sequence, the defender uses a turning kick to ward off his attacker's punch. The defender uses his leg reach because the attacker has chosen to attack with his hands first rather than his legs.

1   Each opponent assumes a stance ready to begin sparring.

2   The attacker (right) steps in to deliver a punch and the defender leans back and prepares to counterattack with a turning kick.

3   As the punch is extended, the defender leans to the side and delivers his turning kick.

1 *The opponents get ready to spar.*

2 *As the attacker (right) attempts a punch, the defender uses his left hand to block it.*

3 *The defender then counters with a reverse punch to the attacker's stomach.*

## Left-hand Block, Reverse Punch to the Stomach

The defender makes a block with his forearm and then a counterattack to the attacker's stomach with a punch.

1 *The sparring partners assume their stances.*

2 *The defender (left) uses his left forearm to block a punch from the attacker.*

97

3 *The defender then quickly delivers an obverse punch with his blocking arm.*

4 *The defender follows the obverse punch with a punch to the attacker's stomach.*

## Left-hand Block, Left-hand Punch to the Face, Right-hand Punch to the Stomach

This is a variation on the previous technique, whereby the defender throws a punch to the face straight after his block, and then follows up with a punch to the stomach.

**1**

**2**

**3**

1 The sparring partners assume their stances.

2 The attacker (left) delivers a side kick with his front leg.

3 The attacker then quickly drops his front leg and follows up with a turning kick from his back leg.

## Side Kick, Turning Kick

This is a combination attack. The first kick used is the side kick. Then, as the side kick finishes, the attacker drops his kicking leg immediately, and his back leg is then used to perform a quick turning kick. These two kicks are usually aimed at the defender's stomach section when being performed.

**1**

**2**

1 The opponents take up their stances ready to spar.

2 The attacker (left) delivers a turning kick with his leading leg.

## Turning Kick, Back Kick

Another combination which involves a turning kick to begin with, which is then followed up by a back kick in order to push the defender backwards, so giving the attacker the option of either backing away or beginning another technique.

**3**

**4**

3 As he finishes the turning kick, the attacker steps his leading leg behind him and gets ready to pivot round.

4 The attacker then immediately delivers a back kick to his opponent's chest or stomach area.

1   The opponents get ready to spar.

2   The attacker (left) steps his rear leg over his front leg.

3   He then delivers a back kick with what is now his rear leg.

4   The attacker drops his leg, while his opponent gets ready to deliver a punch.

5   The attacker performs a side kick with the leg he used for the back kick, preventing his opponent's punch making contact.

## Step-in-Back Kick, Side Kick

Here the attacker uses a step-in-back kick, which enables him to cover distance between himself and the defender, and then easily follow up with a side kick.

1   The sparring partners take up fighting stances.

2   The attacker (left) performs an obverse punch with his left hand.

3   This is then followed up quickly by a reverse hook punch to his opponent's jaw.

## Left Punch to the Face, Right Hook Punch to the Face

A simple punching combination, this sequence entails the attacker throwing a straight left-hand punch to the defender's face, and then following it up with a right hook punch to the defender's jaw or temple, which means the defender has to try to block from two different angles.

Self-defence is the main reason why many people take up a martial art. Taekwon-Do is a martial art which blends self-defence and sport, so people take up Taekwon-Do either because they want to compete in championships and tournaments, or for self-defence purposes. Students need to realise that just because they may be good at sparring and competing, it does not follow that they will be competent in self-defence.

# SELF-DEFENCE

It is important to develop good self-defence skills as your training progresses, along with your other Taekwon-Do skills such as sparring, breaking and pattern work. You need to understand and realise what will and will not work or be applicable in certain situations. For instance, if you are in a crowded room and are attacked, then it will not be possible for you to execute a high section reverse hooking kick! You have to adapt to your surroundings and use different techniques to those that you would if you had a lot of room. So, it is important to have other weapons and techniques in your armoury.

Over the next few pages, you will learn some basic self-defence moves. But just because they are simple it does not mean that they are not effective and, with a bit of practice, you should have no trouble at all in performing them. The moves are mainly techniques to help you escape from various attacks, such as bearhugs, wrist grabs, clothing grabs, headlocks, or being grabbed by the neck, though there are also a couple of punch defences. I decided to make most of them escape techniques, as grabbing someone is the most common way for a fight or an attack to start and I am sure that you would not attack someone for no reason at all.

These techniques are also done principally with the hands, though there are a few knee kicks and some shin and kneecap kicks, because they are particularly effective. In fact, there are a lot of Taekwon-Do self-defence techniques which involve kicks, but they are a bit more complicated to perform, and it will be a while before you start to learn these.

In these situations there are certain areas of the body which you should aim for, particularly if the attacker is at close quarters to you. The vital spots of the human body are called *kupso* in Korean and below are a few of them with their Korean translations:

Neck – *Witmok*
Nose – *Kotdung*
Groin – *Sataguni*
Kneecap/knee joint – *Moorup gwanjol*
Shinbone – *Kyong gol*
Solar Plexus – *Myong chi*
Ribs – *Nuk gol*
Foot – *Pal*
Temple – *Gwanja nori*

1 The attacker grabs the victim by the neck with both hands.

2 The victim then strikes the attacker's ears or temple with her palms.

3 The victim then finishes her defence with a knee kick to the groin.

## Double Neck Grab 1

If you are grabbed round your neck by your attacker, and they are using both hands, then strike with your palms to their ears, or with your knuckles to their temples. Then follow it up with a kick or a knee to the attacker's groin.

1 Again, the attacker grabs the victim's neck with both hands.

2 The victim delivers a kick the attacker's shin bone.

3 She then strikes the underside of the attacker's biceps with her palm.

## Double Neck Grab 2

Another way of freeing yourself when you have been grabbed by an attacker who is using both hands is to kick their shin, or make a hand strike to their ribs. Follow that up with a palm strike to the underside of your attacker's biceps, and then moving either to your right or left, pull yourself out and away from your attacker's grasp.

4 The victim then pulls away from her attacker to the side.

5 The aim is to move away completely from the attacker.

1  *The attacker grabs his victim from behind.*

2  *The victim moves her arm (in this case her right arm) as far forward as possible ready to strike.*

102

3  *The victim can then strike or grab her attacker's groin.*

## Bearhug from Behind 2

Another way to release yourself from a bearhug from behind is to head butt backwards onto your attacker's nose until they let go.

1  *Again, the attacker grabs the victim from behind.*

2  *This time the victim head-butts backwards repeatedly onto her attacker's nose until he releases her.*

## Bearhug from Behind 1

If you are grabbed in a bearhug, then strike with your fist, or grab your attacker's groin.

1 *The attacker grabs his victim from the front.*

2 *The victim performs a knee kick to her attacker's groin to make him release her.*

## Bearhug from the Front 1

If someone grabs you in a bearhug from the front, strike with your knee, up and into your attacker's groin.

1 *Again, the victim is grabbed in a bearhug from the front.*

2 *This time, the victim strikes her attacker's groin with her fist. An alternative is to grab the attacker's groin.*

## Bearhug from the Front 2

Another way of releasing yourself from a bearhug made from the front is either to grab, or make a strike at your attacker's groin.

1    *The attacker grabs the victim in a headlock.*

2    *The victim brings her far arm (in this case the right) round to punch or strike the attacker's groin.*

## Headlock 1

104

If you are caught in a headlock, make a hand strike to, or grab, your attacker's groin.

1    *Again, the victim is grabbed in a headlock.*

2    *The victim then brings her hand round to strike her attacker in the eyes with her fingers.*

## Headlock 2

An alternative release from a headlock is to jab or poke your attacker's eyes, if they are reachable.

1 The attacker grabs his victim by the wrist as she is turning away.

2 The victim turns back towards her attacker.

3 As the attacker pulls the victim towards him, she prepares to bring her knee up.

## Arm Grab 1

If you are walking and somebody grabs you by the arm, pull your arm towards yourself as you turn to face the attacker, then either kick or knee them in the groin. Follow this up with a kick to your attacker's kneecap.

4 The victim then steps through and delivers a kick with her knee to the attacker's groin.

5 She then follows that up with a kick to the attacker's kneecap.

## Arm Grab 2

Another possibility if your arm is grabbed, is to kick your attacker's kneecap straightaway to make them release you.

1 A simple alternative is for the victim to turn quickly as she is grabbed and direct a kick at the attacker's kneecap.

1 *The attacker grabs his victim by her clothing.*

2 *The victim strikes underneath the attacker's elbow joints with her palms.*

3 *She then quickly delivers a kick to the attacker's kneecap.*

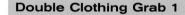

4 *She completes the move by knee kicking the attacker's groin.*

## Double Clothing Grab 1

If your clothes are grabbed by your attacker and he or she is using both hands, palm strike upwards onto their elbow joints, which forces them upwards, and then kick their shin or kneecap, and follow up with a strike to their groin.

1 *Again, the attacker grabs his victim by her clothing with both hands.*

2 *The victim performs a palm strike through her attacker's arms to his nose.*

## Double Clothing Grab 2

An alternative is to bring your arm up through the arms of your attacker (if there is a big enough gap between them) and then palm strike to their nose. Or you could bring your arm round and over your attacker's arms from the outside, and then palm strike them on the nose.

1  *The attacker grabs his victim by both wrists.*

2  *The victim should then pull her arms outwards as far as possible.*

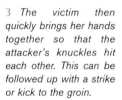

3  *The victim then quickly brings her hands together so that the attacker's knuckles hit each other. This can be followed up with a strike or kick to the groin.*

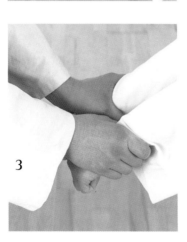

## Double Wrist Grab 1

If both your wrists are grabbed at the same time, relax your arms, then pull them slightly outwards and swing them quickly back inwards, so that your opponent's knuckles are struck together, which should make him (or her) release their grip. To follow up, quickly strike or kick their groin.

## Double Wrist Grab 2

Another defence against this grab is to circle your wrists outwards, grab your attacker with the palms of your hands, and then pull him (or her) towards you and kick or knee them in the groin or stomach.

1  *Again, the attacker grabs his victim's arms.*

107

2  *The victim moves back and gets ready to roll her wrists outwards.*

3  *The victim rolls her wrists and grabs her attacker's wrists, pulling him towards her and executing a front snap kick or front push kick to his groin.*

## Wrist Grab 1

A simple and effective technique to use when your wrist is grabbed is to rotate your wrist in a circular motion outwards, then palm strike your attacker's nose.

1 *The attacker grabs the victim's wrist.*

2 *The victim quickly rotates her wrist outwards.*

3 *As the victim rotates her wrist, she delivers a palm strike to the attacker's nose.*

108

1 *Again, the attacker grabs the victim's wrist.*

2 *This time the victim quickly rotates her wrist to the inside of the attacker's arm.*

3 *As the victim rotates her wrist, she performs a palm strike to her attacker's nose.*

## Wrist Grab 2

The opposite of the previous wrist grab can also be effective. This time you rotate your wrist inwards in a circular motion, and then make a similar palm strike to your attacker's nose.

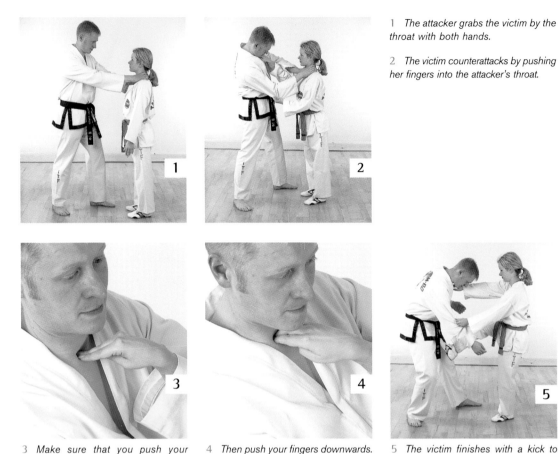

1 The attacker grabs the victim by the throat with both hands.

2 The victim counterattacks by pushing her fingers into the attacker's throat.

3 Make sure that you push your fingers right into the throat.

4 Then push your fingers downwards.

5 The victim finishes with a kick to the attacker's groin.

## Double Neck Grab 3

With this release technique against a double neck grab, you push your thumb or fingers into the throat of your attacker and then downwards. You can also follow this up with a kick to their groin.

1 Again, the attacker grabs the victim by the throat with both hands.

2 The victim turns quickly to her side using her shoulder to break the attacker's grip.

## Double Neck Grab 4

If you are grabbed round the neck by an attacker who is using both hands, turn your shoulder to one side and twist your hips and upper body as you do this to bring your shoulder up slightly so that either it goes through your attacker's arms, or hits his (or her) arm, forcing them to release you.

1 The attacker grabs his victim by the throat with both hands.

2 The victim brings her arm over her attacker's arm and places her thumb under his nose, pushing his head backwards.

## Double Neck Grab 5

110

Another way of achieving a release from a double neck grab, is to put your thumb under the nose, or up the nostril, of your attacker, so forcing their head back. This then gives you the chance to grab their hair and deliver a strike to their throat or neck.

3 The victim then grabs her attacker's hair with her other hand and pulls his head down and to the side.

4 She finishes by delivering a knifehand strike to the victim's exposed neck.

1 The attacker grabs his victim from behind in a bearhug.

2 The victim raises her knee ready to strike.

## Bearhug from Behind 3

If you are grabbed in a bearhug from behind, slide your foot down your attacker's shin, stamp on their foot with your heel, and push your bottom out. This should enable you to turn so that you can aim a kick at your attacker's groin or a strike to their eyes or nose (if you are within range).

3 The victim slides her heel down the attacker's shin bone.

4 The victim then stamps really hard on her attacker's foot.

1  The attacker grabs the victim's wrist.

2  The victim circles her arm over the attacker's arm from the outside inwards.

## Arm Grab 3

If your arm is grabbed, bring your forearm underneath and back over your attacker's arm, and push down with your forearm onto his or her elbow joint. Pull your opponent towards you with your forearm, while still trying to press down on their elbow with your forearm. You should then be able to deliver a strike to their throat or solar plexus from this position and follow it up with a knee kick to their groin.

3  The victim presses her forearm down onto the attacker's elbow joint, forcing him to lose his grip.

4  As the victim continues to push down with her forearm, she delivers a knifehand strike to the attacker's neck.

1 *The attacker grabs the victim's wrist.*

2 *The victim rolls her wrist outwards over the attacker's arm.*

3 *The victim then rolls her arm back over the attacker's arm.*

4 *The victim steps to the side of the attacker as she brings her arm onto the top of his shoulder.*

5 *The victim locks her free arm onto her other hand which is now on the attacker's shoulder and then forces the attacker downwards.*

6 *The victim then delivers a knee kick to the attacker's face.*

## Wrist Grab 3

This release from a wrist grab involves quickly circling your wrist from the outside to the inside of your attacker's forearm. You then repeat it and, as you do so, move to the side of your opponent. From here your hand should come underneath your attacker's shoulder, and then you place it on top of the shoulder. Lock your other hand onto that hand and force your opponent's arm and shoulder down to the floor (dropping your body weight onto your nearest leg forces your attacker downwards more quickly).

1   *The attacker grabs the victim in a headlock.*

2   *The victim pushes her forearm upwards into her attacker's throat.*

## Headlock 3

If you are caught in a headlock, put your hand up and push your attacker's chin or nose backwards. As you do this, turn your body in the direction of the arm which you are using and turn yourself round. From this position, you can turn to make a hand strike to your attacker's throat or eyes.

3   *The victim turns round as she continues to push her forearm into the attacker's throat.*

4   *With her forearm still pushing into the attacker's throat and thus off balance, she administers a palm strike to his nose.*

*The attacker aims a hook punch at the victim who blocks it with her outer forearm.*

2 *The victim then steps towards her attacker and delivers a palm strike to his nose.*

## Hook Punch 1

If your attacker swings a punch at you, block with your outer forearm making sure that your fist is clenched, and step forward performing a palm strike to the nose of your attacker. Then place your foot behind your attacker's leading leg and strike with your front elbow to their throat or upper chest region. This should force them downwards to the floor.

115

3 *Finally, the victim makes an elbow strike to her attacker's chest with the same arm she used to deliver the palm strike.*

1 *The attacker aims a hook punch at the victim who blocks it with a double forearm block.*

## Hook Punch 2

If your attacker swings a hook punch towards you, block with both your forearms (hands in clenched fists) and then with your nearest hand perform an inward knifehand strike to your attacker's neck. Follow this up with a front elbow strike to their nose.

2 *The victim then strikes the attacker's neck with a knifehand, using the nearest hand for speed.*

3 *The victim follows the knifehand with an elbow strike to the attacker's nose.*

116

1   *The attacker grabs the victim by the wrist.*

2   *The victim quickly turns her body and pulls her arm to the opposite side.*

## Wrist Grab 4

Another defence against a wrist grab is to pull your arm quickly to one side and then to the other to release your opponent's hold. From here, you can follow up with a kick to their groin, shin or kneecap.

3   *She then turns the other way quickly, pulling her arm back.*

4   *In so doing, the victim should pull her arm free of her attacker's grasp.*

1 The attacker grabs the victim by her clothes.

2 The victim brings her arms over the attacker's and grabs his arm on the far side.

3 The victim then turns her body over in the opposite direction.

4 As she does so, the victim rolls her over both of her attacker's arms.

5 The victim now has both of her attacker's arms trapped under her arm.

6 The victim can now turn and deliver an elbow strike to her attacker's face.

## Double Clothing Grab 3

A defence against a double clothing grab, that is when someone grabs your clothes with both hands, is to bring your furthest arm and hand over your attacker's arms to grab their far hand and pull it towards your far side while you put your other arm and hand over your attacker's arms. As you do this, turn your body away and towards the side you are pulling your attacker. Try to lock your hand on the attacker's hand, as you lock your other arm over the top of both their arms.

This technique needs to be done fast, and with a turn, so you will end up twisting your attacker round and locking their arms together. After this, you can turn yourself back the other way to deliver an elbow strike to their face or neck and, as you turn, your attacker's grip should be released.

1 *The attacker grabs the victim's wrist.*

## Wrist Grab 5

Another release from a wrist grab is to roll your wrist from the inside to the outside of your attacker's hold and then strike with your forearm upwards to the underside of the elbow of the arm with which your attacker has grabbed you while you step to the side. From here, make a palm strike to their nose or throat, or kick them in their groin.

2 *The victim steps forward and strikes under the elbow of the arm that the attacker is using to hold her with her forearm.*

3 *The victim then delivers a palm strike to the attacker's face. Alternatively she can kick her attacker's groin with her knee.*

# RELAXING AFTER A SESSION

Obviously as you train, you maintain a high level of adrenaline and excitement during the lesson, and you will probably find it hard to come down afterwards, so the last 5–10 minutes of a class should be used to relax.

A warming-down period of a class may consist of any of the following:

## Light stretching exercises

These constitute a good way to warm down, as by the end of a class your muscles are very warm, and you will be more flexible. Of course, you can do some stretching on your own, but at the end of a lesson it is a good idea to use a partner, because then you can do more advanced stretches with their help.

As you perform your stretches, talk to your partner to tell them how far you can extend in a certain stretch and make sure that he or she eases you either into or out of the stretch.

Here are some typical stretching routines for warming down which you can practise on your own:

1  Sit on the floor and extend your legs in front of you. Keep them straight and together, and take a deep breath in, then slowly breathe out, as you bring your forehead down to your knees. You can also try to reach your toes with your hands, and either hold your ankles, or the balls of your feet.

2  Sit on the floor and extend your left leg straight in front of you and tuck the other leg in towards the thigh muscle of the extended leg. Once more, try to reach and hold the ball of the foot on your extended leg with your right hand. As you do this, try to put your forehead onto your knees. Change legs and repeat the exercise. You should try and do it a few times with each leg extended.

3  Sitting down again, extend your legs out to your sides (as far as you can). Try to keep your legs straight and don't raise them off the floor (this stretch is known as a split stretch). Put your hands on the floor in front of you and slowly 'walk' yourself forwards.

4   Stand with one leg forwards, and extend your other leg back. Keeping your hands on your hips, lower your body down slightly and then lower the knee of your rear leg further so that it is a few inches off the floor. Hold the stretch and try not to let your knee touch the floor. Change legs and repeat the exercise. Try to do it several times for each leg.

5   Standing straight, slowly lower your body forwards and try to bring your chest and your forehead towards your knees. Support the backs of your knees with your hands as you do this stretch.

6   Again, stand straight and take one of your legs over the front of the other, keeping both feet firmly on the floor. Then slowly lower your body forwards, until you reach your limit, and hold the stretch for a few seconds. Change legs and repeat the stretch.

7   Standing straight, take your left arm right across your chest. Push your right forearm onto your left elbow, so that your left arm comes towards you and you feel a stretch in the top of your left arm. Hold the position for a few seconds and then change arms and repeat it. This stretch is good for the arms and upper chest.

8   Once again standing straight, take one arm behind your back and bend it upwards with the palm of the hand facing outwards. Keep it flat against your back as you bring your other arm over your shoulder and down your back until you can hold your hands together. Then pull down with the lower arm. Change arms and repeat. You may not be able to do both, but keep practising!

9   Standing straight, balance on one leg and lift your other leg up behind you and hold onto the foot. This is a good stretch for your thigh muscles and it also helps to improve your balance. You can then try to extend the leg you are holding to the side and also to the front of you, locking it out straight as you do so.

10   Circle your head very slowly clockwise a few times, then do the same in an anti-clockwise direction. Bring your head forwards, so that your chin touches your chest, and then lean your head backwards, so the back of your head touches the base of your neck. Finally, tilt your head slowly from side to side.

11   Slowly roll your arms in large circles, gradually decreasing the size of the circles. This exercise helps to relax your shoulders and ease the tightness out of them from punching and hand techniques.

## Breathing exercises

As you train, depending on how the lesson is structured, you may run out of breath a little and find yourself breathing harder than normal. After you have completed an exercise and are resting, try to remember to breathe in through your nose and out through your mouth, which will help you control the rhythm of your breathing. When you are doing a warm-down, try to breathe much more shallowly than you usually would. Breathe in from the pit of your stomach, through your nose and then very slowly all the way out through your mouth.

## Light massaging

Again, as with stretching, you can either do this on your own, or with a partner. A good way to massage is for you to lie on your stomach and let another student gently perform light knifehand strikes to your calf muscles, thighs, back and arms. Once this is done, lie on your back, and get your partner to do the same again to your thighs and arms. You would then do the same for your partner.

If you are massaging your own muscles, then just knead them lightly all over to relieve them of stress. After you have finished doing a massage exercise, always shake your body out. In other words, relax your body and shake your arms and hands, circle your head slowly round one way and then another, shake your legs out and circle your ankles and knees.

## Meditation exercises

You must relax your body completely, concentrate and focus to be able to do this. People often sit cross-legged on the floor, or with their feet tucked under them and close their eyes. Once you are doing this, try to imagine something in your mind's eye, or concentrate on a noise that you may hear, your instructor's footsteps as they walk round the hall, for example, or maybe another student's breathing. Control your breathing and try to make it shallow.

## Performing your *tul* (pattern)

Another way to warm down is to perform your respective *tul* (pattern) very slowly. Sometimes referred to as dynamic pattern work, it is a good way to relax and also helps you to control your breathing correctly. During the *tul* you concentrate on your techniques, such as punches, blocks, strikes and kicks, and your stances, which helps improve your balance. Many students find that doing this is in itself a form of meditation, as a lot of focus and concentration are required.

These are just some of the more typical ways of warming down. Of course, different instructors teach different things, and some schools may not make too much of it, though most instructors agree that it is a very important part of the lesson. Occasionally, an instructor will read from a book to explain more about different aspects of Taekwon-Do, such as its history or about a technique. Alternatively, he or she may get you to sit down and then ask you questions from the school's syllabus to see how much of it you know.

123

# FURTHER
# INFORMATION

The following may be of help, if you want to find out more about Taekwon-Do, its history and the various organisations that exist to govern and promote it.

## Recommended books

Choi, General Hong Hi, *Taekwon-Do*, ITF, South Korea, 1st edition 1988, 3rd edition 1999. Fifteen volumes. (The ultimate reference work on Taekwon-Do which includes the history of the martial arts, step-by-step instructions on all the techniques, diagrams of each of the 24 *tuls* (patterns), information about gradings and competitions, training secrets etc.)

Choi, General Hong Hi, *Taekwon-Do: The Condensed Encyclopedia*, ITF, Korea, 5th edition 1999. (A condensed version of the 15-volume encyclopedia, which concentrates quite heavily on each of the patterns, and also on self-defence techniques.)

Hee, Master Il Cho, *The Complete Taekwon-Do Hyung*, Cho's Taekwon-Do Publishing House, USA, 1988. Three volumes. (Hyung is sometimes used instead of *tul* and also translates as 'pattern'. These books include step-by-step photographs of all 24 patterns.)

*Other training aids*

## Videos

There are various videos available. I recommend *Taekwon-Do – Korean art of self-defence* by former World ITF champion Henk Meyer. He guides you through various warm-up exercises, punches, kicks, pad work, sparring techniques and some body conditioning. The video shows a lot of the techniques in slow motion so you can see the correct execution of the technique.

## CD roms

General Choi has also released a set of four CD roms called *Legacy*, containing all the information from his encyclopedia in visual form, such as step-by-step instructions on the techniques. There is a Korean interpreter who recites over two hundred Korean phrases and words, so you can learn how to pronounce the terminology correctly and learn their translations. There is a section called 'Ask the General', a compilation of video clips, in which General Choi himself gives answers to questions on Taekwon-Do and the martial arts.

*If you would like to contact the International Taekwon-Do Federation,*
*the address of their headquarters is:*

International Taekwon-Do Federation
Drau Gasse 3
A-1210 Vienna
Austria (ITF)

Telephone: (+43 1) 292 84 67
Facsimile:  (+43 1) 292 55 09

There is also a web site for the ITF: www.itf-taekwondo.com

*The United Kingdom Taekwon-Do Association can be contacted*
*at the following address:*

PO Box 162
Orpington
Kent BR6 0WU

Telephone: (+44) (0)1689 812888
Facsimile: (+44) (0)1689 813895

*The United States Taekwon-Do Federation can be contacted*
*at the following address:*

6801 W 117th Avenue E-5
Broomfield
CO 80020

Telephone: (+1) 303 466 4963

125

# GLOSSARY

**An bakat palmok kaundae makgi** – inner forearm middle block (see page 41)

**An suroh chagi** – inner sweep (see page 78)

**Annun sogi** – sitting stance (see page 22)

**Ap** – front (of the body)

**Ap cha busigi** – front snap kick (see page 37)

**Ap cha milgi** – front push kick (see page 76)

**Ap cha mum chagi** – front checking kick (see page 69)

**Ap cha olligi** – front rising kick (see page 80)

**Ap joomuk** – forefist (front part of the fist)

**Bakat palmok kaundae makgi** – outer forearm middle block (see page 42)

**Bakat sonkal terrigi** – outer knifehand strike (see page 59)

**Bakat suroh chagi** – outer sweep (see page 79)

**Baldung** – instep

**Balkut** – toes

**Bandae** – reverse

**Bandae bandal chagi** – reverse crescent kick (see page 74)

**Bandae dollyo chagi** – reverse turning kick (see page 35)

**Bandae gorro chagi** – reverse hooking kick (see page 39)

**Bandae jurugi** – reverse punch (see page 27)

**Bandal chagi** – crescent kick (see page 73)

**Baro** – obverse

**Baro jurugi** – obverse punch (see page 28)

**Bituro chagi** – twisting kick (see page 75)

**Chagi** – kick

**Charyiot** – attention

**Charyot sogi** – attention stance (see page 23)

**Chookyo makgi** – rising block (see page 43)

**Chunbi** – ready

**Dobok** – training suit

**Do-jang** – training hall

**Dollyo chagi** – turning kick (see page 34)

**Dollyo jurugi** – hook punch (see page 29)

**Dom joomuk** – back fist

**Doo palmok makgi** – double forearm block (see page 84)

**Doro chagi** – waving kick (see page 81)

**Dwijibo jurugi** – upset punch (see page 31)

**Dwit** – back

**Dwit cha chagi** – back kick (see page 36)

**Dwit kumchi** – heel base

**Dwitbal sogi** – rear foot stance (see page 49)

**Dwitchuk** – back heel

**Goburyo sogi** – bending stance (see page 51)

**Gojung sogi** – fixed stance (see page 50)

**Gorro chagi** – hooking kick (see page 38)

**Gunnun sogi** – walking stance (see page 21)

**Jeja** – student

**Joomuk** – fist

**Jurugi** – punch

**Kaeundae** – middle section (of body)

**Kunya** – bow

**Kyocha chookyo makgi** – 'X' fist rising block (see page 82)

**Kyocha naeryo makgi** – 'X' fist downward block (see page 83)

**Kyocha sogi** – 'X' stance (see page 48)

**Makgi** – block

**Matsogi** – sparring

**Miro makgi** – pushing block (see page 85)

**Moa sogi** – close stance (see page 53)

**Mumchau makgi** – checking block (see page 88)

**Moorup** – knee

**Moorup chagi** – knee kick (see page 77)

**Naeryo chagi** – axe kick (see page 68)

**Naeryo makgi** – downward block (see page 47)

**Najundae** – low section (of body)

**Narani junbi sogi** – parallel ready stance (see page 24)

**Niunja sogi** – 'L' stance (see page 25)

**Nopundae** – high section (of body)

**Oguryo sogi** – crouched stance (see page 54)

**Ollyo jurugi** – uppercut punch (see page 56)

**Oron** – right

**Pal** – foot

**Palkop** – elbow

**Palkop terrigi** – elbow strike

**Palmok daebi makgi** – forearm guarding block (see page 46)

**Sabumnim** – instructor

**Sang palmok makgi** – twin forearm block (see page 87)

**Sho** – relax

**Sijut** – start

**Son** – hand

**Sonbadak** – palm (of hand)

**Sonbadak gorro makgi** – palm hooking block (see page 86)

**Sonbadak ollyo makgi** – palm upward block (see page 89)

**Sonbadak terrigi** – palm strike (see page 57)

**Sonkal** – knifehand

**Sonkal daebi makgi** – knifehand guarding block (see page 45)

**Sonkal makgi** – knifehand block (see page 44)

**Sonkal terrigi** – inner knifehand strike (see page 58)

**Sonkut** – fingertips

**Soojik sogi** – vertical stance (see page 52)

**Sun jurugi** – straight line punch (see page 65)

**Terrigi** – strike

**Tti** – belt

**Twigi** – jumping

**Twigi dwit cha chagi** – jump back kick (see page 72)

**Twigi yop chagi** – jump side kick (see page 71)

**Yop** – side

**Yop cha mum chagi** – side checking kick (see page 70)

**Yop chagi** – side kick (see page 33)

**Yop jurugi** – side punch (see page 30)

**Wen** – left

126

# INDEX

# INDEX